D1576459

Dressing the Colonised Body

Politics, Clothing and Identity in Sri Lanka

Dressing the Colonised Body

Politics, Clothing and Identity in Sri Lanka

NIRA WICKRAMASINGHE

Orient Longman

ORIENT LONGMAN PRIVATE LIMITED

Registered Office
3-6-752 Himayatnagar, Hyderabad 500 029 (A.P.), INDIA

Other Offices
Bangalore, Bhopal, Bhubaneshwar, Chennai, Ernakulam,
Guwahati, Hyderabad, Jaipur, Kolkata, Lucknow,
Mumbai, New Delhi, Patna

© Orient Longman Private Limited 2003

ISBN 81 250 2479 4

Typeset by
OSDATA
Hyderabad

Printed at
Baba Barkha Nath Printers
New Delhi

Published by
Orient Longman Private Limited
1/24 Asaf Ali Road, New Delhi 110 002

CONTENTS

Chapter One

Introduction

'The body . . . cannot escape being a vehicle of history, a metaphor and metonym of being-in-time'.[1]

The colonised body is beautifully evoked in the photograph that I borrowed from *Twentieth-Century Impressions of Ceylon* (1907) as a cover for my book: an old blacksmith burned by the sun, his dark and bare body sweltering, covered only with a dirty cloth wrapped around his waist, barefoot, working hard. On his head, a bowler hat.

In the essays that compose *Dressing the Colonised Body*, popular, political and economic meanings assigned to clothing and dress are explored in a variety of colonial contexts. Although most examples come from Sri Lanka, I have attempted to draw from other Asian and African sources too. I try to capture some historical dimensions to the body in society. Indeed, major political and personal problems are often problematised in the body, dressed or undressed, and expressed through it.

In recent years there has been a widened body of research on the body surface as a principal site of social and political action by feminists and scholars in the field of cultural studies. In their works, dress is considered as both sign and commodity enmeshed in multiple webs of meaning and value. They deal with the relationship between the body and society, the issue of embodiment in relation to theories of social action, the body and feminist theory, and the body in consumer culture. Like Roach and Eicher, Cordwell and Schwartz, Appadurai, Weiner and Schneider, Barnes and Eicher and others, I hope to bring to the discussion of cloth/clothing/dress cross-cultural insights from the increasingly intertwined fields of anthropology and history.[2] But the essays in this volume do not adopt the same writing 'strategy'; they refuse opaque language games, and try, instead, to be readable without being vacuous.

Dress and sartorial trends are part of a long-term debate on identity and modernity which is played out at different levels of society from the village to the nation. Dress and clothing are not only important comments upon the existent; they also transmit a variety of cultural meanings. Dress touches on every issue—raw material, production processes, manufacturing costs, cultural stability, fashion and social hierarchy. Clothes are never innocent or simply functional; they 'signify', as Ferdinand de Saussure would have said.

Clothing is very much a social artefact. In most non-western cultures men and women show tremendous creativity in the adornment of their body by means of clothes, paints or jewellery. The body becomes the bearer of cultural signs. Dress is thus a mode of non-verbal communication, if not a language, at least a system of signification. Thus, Braudel thinks of fashion as an indication of the energies, possibilities, demands and joie de vivre of a given society, economy and civilisation.

The study of dress may appear to be a mundane area of research. It can, however, show the way in which people seek to manage and express their identity. Clothes permit the wearer to play with his or her identity. They are often used to define, to present, to deceive, to reveal and conceal. What is interesting is why people make certain choices of dress. Dressing is as much a creative act as a political act. Clothes are often considered extensions of the people who wear them. Cloth too is now understood to have considerable semiotic value in the expression of both the fragility and the potency of social statuses and socio-political relations. It is critical in the representation and reproduction of society and forms a crucial link between social groups across space and through time.

The period of Sri Lanka's history that I focus my attention on has been the subject of many books and essays. Issues such as the incipient nationalist movement, the plantation industry, the colonisation of land in the dry zone in the late nineteenth century and early twentieth century have inspired historians to offer interesting and varied interpretations. More recently, studies of particular events of the period which conventional historians would consider unimportant have brought some piquant flavour to the staid history-writing of Sri Lanka. Using colonial sources and reading them anew, Michael Roberts, has on many occasions attempted, but with unequal success, to follow the subaltern studies historians' mode of exegesis. His study of 'noise' is, nevertheless, path-breaking.[3] Anthropological studies emphasising gender issues have also looked at new subject areas such as domesticity, but their reliance on Christian missionary writings as sources highlights the historian's difficulty in finding out what the objects of inquiry, those written about, actually thought.[4]

The second essay in *Dressing the Colonised Body* uses dress as a mode of entering the *mentalites* of the people to whom power was transferred in 1948. The third charts the changes in production and consumption of cloth and textile and the advent of the sewing machine in the early twentieth century, changes which in many ways embody the encounter of Sri Lanka with modernity. The fourth essay captures the ways in which colonial minds constructed authenticity and the different ways colonised bodies responded. The fifth chapter, perhaps the most ambitious, attempts to recreate, through three photographs, the life of a man through a study of his dress. Studying the vagaries of dress during this period of nationalism is perhaps a way of feeling and sensing rather than acquiring a cognitive understanding of the nation-state as it emerged after colonialism.

The question of how to reconstruct past systems of meaning, when one can neither participate nor directly observe the lives of the people, has preoccupied historians for a number of decades. In France, historians have attempted to write a history of *mentalités* by drawing on new types of evidence such as visual imagery and oral traditions and also digging deeper into sources of information authors did not consciously impart. To write history is for me, among many other things, to recreate in a certain way, selectively and intuitively, a particular period and how it felt to live during this period. One of the historian's most daunting challenges has been to recreate the mentalities of people and individuals who did not leave any traces, or if they did, left problematic traces. As Amin comments:

> Peasants do not write, they are written about. The speech of humble folk is not normally recorded for posterity; it is wrenched from them in courtrooms and inquisitorial trials. Historians have therefore learnt to comb 'confessions' and 'testimonies' for their evidence, for this is where peasants cry out, dissimulate or indeed narrate.[5]

Social historians have read between the lines of the writings of the literati surmising occasional clues. Mentalites, as an object of inquiry, was superbly adopted by Robert Darnton, a specialist of France in the Ancien Regime especially in his book *The Great Cat Massacre and other Episodes in French Cultural History*. He suggested that by picking at the document where it is most opaque, we may be able to unravel an alien system of meaning. If you find the thread, it might lead you into a strange and wonderful world-view. The mode of exegesis may vary but in each case one reads for meaning—the meaning inscribed by contemporaries in what- ever survives of their visions of the world. In this way, his approach is very close to that of anthropologists who try to see things from the native's point of view, to understand what he/she means and to seek the social dimensions of meaning. For Darnton and other social historians, the purpose of history-writing is to put together symbolic worlds that collapsed centuries ago. The method used is the working back and forth between texts and contexts. As Darnton writes:

> ... the mental world of the unenlightened during the Enlightenment seems to be irretrievably lost ... [and for this reason] the historian must resemble the ogre of the legend when he ventures into the past to try to make contact with vanished humanity.[6]

The first step is to let the documents breathe and listen to their murmur.

In these essays I interrogate dress, for dress is the language of the non-literate, the mute and the liar. If people cannot or do not speak, their bodies always do. But their bodies can also lie, or dissimulate, take you down false roads, play with your perceptions. Dress alone is not reliable as a source or as a text. The historian, if he or she is to succeed in reconstructing symbolic worlds, must move to and fro from text to context and display a certain amount of critical disbelief.

This book has many heritages, and is partly borne out of disappointments. For one, a certain disappointment with the Subaltern Studies approach to nationalism and culture which completely leaves out from their consideration material culture such as clothing, food, habitat, and fails to show how material culture is produced by human agency in the process of social interaction. Second, a certain disappointment with the approach of the French historians of the *Lieux de memoire*, a collective enterprise guided by Pierre Nora that aimed at charting the places where a society deposits its memories; these places could be topographical, monumental, symbolic or functional.[7] While material culture is present in these writings what they lack is a narrative that gives them life. Memories belong to people and even though, as Thucydides reminds us, they forget, deform and obey a pleasure economy, their quality comes from their subjective nature. The fact that dress—whether national dress or regional costume—is not present among the selected lieux de memoire, is in my view an eye-opener on the reluctance of mainstream scholars to address issues which deal with the body.

When researching this book, I combined archival data with the insights of a wide range of living speakers—men and women, young and old—to illuminate both the present and the past. Photographs and advertisements too were pertinent to the exploration and understanding of the cultural systems of the time. Most of these were not included in the book, but form its nervous system, as it were.

6

This study would not have been possible if not for the SEPHIS post-doctoral grant I received in 1996–97. I am very grateful to the SEPHIS board and to Dr Ulbe Bosma for helping me realise a project which had little chances of taking off in these times of policy-oriented research. I hope the reader finds in these pages something enjoyable as well as interesting.

Nira Wickramasinghe

NOTES

1. J. L. Comaroff and J. Comaroff. 'Bodily Reform as Historical Practice'. In J. L. Comaroff and J. Comaroff (eds.) *Ethnography and the Historical Imagination*, Boulder, Colorado, Westview, 1992: 79.

2. A. Appadurai (ed.) *The Social Life of Things: Commodities in Cultural Perspective*. New York: Cambridge University Press; R. Barness and J. Eicher (eds.) *Dress and Gender: Making and Meaning*. Providence: R.I. Berg, 1992; M. Cordwell and R.A. Schwartz (eds.) *The Fabrics of Culture: The Anthropology of Clothing and Adornment*. The Hague: Mouton, 1979; M.E. Roach and J.B. Eicher (eds.) *Dress, Adornment and the Social Order*. New York: John Wiley and Sons, 1965; A. Weiner and J. Schneider (ed.) *Cloth and Human Experience*. Washington D.C., Smithsonian Institute Press, 1989.

3. Michael Roberts. 'The Imperialism of Silence under the British Raj: Arresting the Drum' In M. Roberts (ed.) *Exploring Confrontation. Sri Lanka: Politics, Culture and History*. Chur. Switzerland: Harwood Academic Publishers, 1994: 149–81.

4. Malathi de Alwis. 'The Production and Embodiment of Respectability: Gendered Demeanours in Colonial Ceylon'. In Michael Roberts (ed.) *Sri Lanka. Collective Identities Revisited: Vol. I.* Colombo Marga Institute, 1997: 105–44.
5. Shahid Amin. *Event, Metaphor, Memory: Chauri Chaura 1922– 1992.* New Delhi, Oxford University Press, 1995: 1.
6. Robert Darnton. *The Great Cat Massacre and Other Episodes in French Cultural History.* New York: Vintage Books, 1985.
7. Pierre Nora (ed.) *Les Lieux de Mémoire.* Paris: Gallimard, 1997.

Chapter Two

INDEPENDENCE AND
THE NATIONAL DRESS

Tout commemoration vit de l'affirmation obsessive du meme
Mona Ozouf

It was dressed in top hat and tails that the first Prime Minister of independent Ceylon, D.S. Senanayake hoisted the Lion Flag on 10 December 1948 when the inauguration of the new Parliament took place.

D.S. Senanayake, born on 20 October 1884 at Botale near Mirigama of a 'respectable' and wealthy family, was the third son of Don Spater Senanayake, landowner and plumbago merchant. His father and uncles who were active in the incipient nationalist movement had been imprisoned by the

British after the 1915 anti-Muslim riots. He was educated at St Thomas's College, an Anglican public school where, if he did not display a predilection for studies, he blossomed into a fine athlete.

The British chose him as a successor to devolve power from among a few acceptable aspirants. His enduring quality was perhaps his appeal as a moderate statesman. In many ways the transfer of power was officiated by a few men in bowler hats. Among D.S. Senanayake's mentors and advisers was Sir Ivor Jennings. Together they steered Ceylon along the path of modernity. The instrument of power was a fledgling political party called the United National Party, especially created for the 1947 elections with the support of the colonial rulers. The party had the singular objective of ensuring that communism did not take a foothold in Ceylon. In that sense Senanayake was the epitome of a bourgeois modernity that contrasted with the radical and progressive modernities of the left wing parties.

Senanayake wore the dress of his class. In 1948, an elegant man would wear a Cantex banian and over it a Gable self-coloured or striped shirt. He would wear a leather belt with a plated buckle and Oxford shoes.[1]

This image of a man in bowler hat, an image full of para-doxes, cannot fade from people's memories as it appears every year on the front page of newspapers commemorating the event. Through this single act of staging, the idea of the Ceylonese polity had been expressed in bodily symbolism, as a polity which was reluctant to evoke even symbolically its detachment from colonial rule. The reason was so simple and transparent that one feared to even utter it: Ceylon did not rebel, she acquiesced to colonial rule. But was it so simple? Were the Ceylonese nothing else than 'an essentially imitative people' with little they could call their own? Hugh Clifford described them in the following terms:

> they have adopted from their childhood the manner of living, the speech and as many of the social usages of the English as their means can make accessible to them. They are proud of having imbibed such an exclusive British quality as the public school spirit . . . and they display a no less British extrava-gance in the keen interest they take in games, none of which

is indigenous . . . and in their admiration of athletic prowess. They delight in public banquets . . . attend them clad in orthodox evening dress.[2]

What Hugh Clifford, who had a sensibility of his time, could not perceive was that the 'native culture' and the West were mutually engaged in a semiotic web whose implications were not completely controlled by the protagonists. It is through these performative processes, critical to the creation of tradition and modernity, that national identity was negotiated. Looking at dress at a particular time—the moment of independence, where self-representation is at its peak—permits us to conceive the lineages that exist between the colonial past and the present. It permits us to enter the mind of the men to whom power was transferred on that day which is commemorated every year and has become known as the 'National Day' or 'Independence Day'.

A national day speaks to our imagination. It serves as an index of the dominant discourse of power and politics. But people live it in other ways subverting the hegemonic discourse, wrapping it in their own meanings.

What I hope to suggest is that behind the top hat and tails of the leaders, other people were experimenting with modernity through dress, and living independence through modes of perception which had little to do with the official state approach. Unlike the character in Clifford's description, they either offered some resistance or partook willingly and consciously in the march of modernity.

Experimenting With a New Idiom: The Invention of a National Dress

It is possible to imagine D.S. Senanayake wearing a different outfit at the independence ceremonies for a few decades before the contour of a national dress had been drawn and some political leaders had began to wear it at official functions. The idea of a national dress which would be worn by men of all classes and communities—women were still not included in the realm of the political-symbolic—emerged in the early twentieth century as a reaction to the adoption of a western style of dress by many natives. In South Asia, this western dress was not consciously imposed upon the people by the colonisers whether Portuguese, Dutch or British. In fact, at first European conquerors did not in many instances dream of propagating, much less imposing, European forms of life on foreign peoples in tropical countries; rather they tended to adopt the latter's styles of life and particularly dress which they realised were better suited to local conditions. French Jesuit missionaries, for instance, in Southern India emulated Brahmin dress.[3] But soon European styles of dress became prestige symbols among non-Europeans and this led to the adoption by elite groups of a dark formal dress of a type completely unsuited to the climatic conditions of the country. In Ceylon, western clothes were a status symbol to the extent that Europeans began to feel that the native dress, when worn in an ostentatious manner, was symbolic of disobedience or was at any rate contrary to the demand for submission to the superior colonial power and to Christian demeanour.[4]

11

The situation was quite unlike that in India. In Bengal for instance, foreign clothing was considered impure and shed by its male wearer before he went into the inner apartments of his home. While many Indians admired Europe's scientific discoveries and educational standards, they were often critical of other aspects of European culture and remained highly selective over which elements should be adopted or absorbed into Indian life. Clothes were among the many manifestations of British culture which were carefully assessed and partly assimilated by a small but influential Indian elite. Since clothing had always been an important sign of affiliation to different social and religious groups in India, few people were prepared to abandon their raiment of identity overnight. Unlike in Ceylon, a vast proportion of the rural population and almost all the female population in India continued to dress in predominantly Indian styles throughout the period of British rule.

In the middle and late nineteenth century, at the time Christianity was winning over new converts and European values were getting entrenched in Ceylon, a powerful religio-cultural challenge appeared in the form of a Buddhist revivalist movement. Its leadership was constituted of educated Sinhala Buddhists and of monks from the Sinhalese Low-Country, the most famous being Mohottivatte Gunananda. Its protest was on three fronts: it sought primarily to refute the aggressive claims of Christianity, to create a modern Buddhist system of schools, and to encourage abstinence. A few decades earlier, a Hindu revival, inspired by the Hindu religious revival in India, was brought into being in the north of the country by men such as Arumugam Navalar and by organisations such as the Saiva Paripalana Sabhai. The Buddhist and Hindu revivalist movements were not simple and distinct social movements, rather they blended several actions and personalities. Recent scholarship has established that Navalar, whose works and acts focussed essentially on Saivite revival and were restricted to the Vellala caste, was no social reformer, and in this sense differed from the leaders of the Buddhist movement led by the newly emergent middle-class who challenged the social values of Christianity and British rule as a whole.[5] Indeed, continuous Christian activity since the arrival of the Portuguese had created a community of Christianised Ceylonese who looked down upon Buddhism, Hinduism and Islam.

The contest over clothing was in many ways symptomatic of the wider contest that was taking place between Christianity and Buddhism. A similar contest was happening in Africa. In the last decade of the nineteenth and the early twentieth centuries, as the Church sought to establish mission stations in French Congo, clothing was essential in signifying the success of evangelism, as a means of teaching values and in the identity of the first African Christians. Conversion involved the transformation of the whole person, the creation of a new human being. Monseigneur Carrie, first Bishop of the Loango Mission of the Holy Ghost Fathers, wrote in 1890:

> ... Moral training is more important than the intellectual training of children. It is not enough to teach religion but to create men who can live in society.[6]

In the early twentieth century, the social and religious reformers, Anagarika Dharmapala and Walisinha Harischandra led a campaign to protect places of Buddhist worship. They were also leaders of the Temperance movement. This endeavour which had two peaks, one in 1903–05 and a more important one in 1911–14, had a dual purpose: first to reiterate Buddhist strictures against alcohol which amounted to the assertion anew of the validity and relevance of Buddhist values after years of acquiescence to the values of the foreign rulers; second, (and on a more temporal plane) it represented on the political plane a move to attack the excise policy as an important source of British revenue. The impact of this movement was not confined to the urban intelligentsia but spread to the rural middle-class and to the urban workers through the new Sinhala theatre of John de Silva for instance, where anti-colonial themes formed the core of the sub-narrative. Dharmapala himself played a crucial role in the propagation of ideas emphasising Sinhalese culture as a historically composite identity which in his view could only be Buddhist. The 'Lion Race' and the Sinhalese nation was the hub of his thinking which had originated from a mythologising of history and a retrospective romanticism.

13

Dress reform was part of Dharmapala's programme to restore a Sinhalese pride in their culture.

> We are blindly following the white man who has come here to demoralise for his own gain. He asks us to buy his whisky, and we allow him to bamboozle us. He tells us that we should drink toddy and arrack separately, that we should teach our children Latin and Greek and keep them in ignorance of our own beautiful literature and that we should think like the Yorkshire man and not like our own Dutugemunu and Parakramabahu and Sirisangbodhi, and that we should discard our own national dress which was good for our noble and spirited ancestors, and dress according to the dictates of the fashion of London and Paris.[7]

Clearly the 'national dress' was in the mind of men such as Dharmapala, the dress of the Sinhalese man who would partake in public life. Men's dress as defined by Dharmapala was very much a Sinhalese dress reminiscent of the dress worn by the kings Dutugemunu and Parakramabahu and which contrasted favourably with the dress of other ethnic groups:

> The Sinhalese dress is complete if instead of the sarong, trousers, combs etc., presently worn by the Sinhalese one wears a white

or silk cloth, a long banian with a shawl over it, hair cut short, a headband made of flimsy cloth on the head and a pair of shoes for the feet. The rich can wear varieties of silk cloth, ornaments embedded with gold, pearl and gems for the head, a necklace for the neck and a pair of beautiful shoes made with gold thread.[8]

The Sinhalese man should abide by the following rules. He

Should not show the entire body like the Veddas who wear only a loincloth.
Should not wear trousers like the fair Portuguese.
Should not wear combs on the head like the Batavian Malays.
Should not wear a hat wrapped in cloth, comb, collar, tie, banian, shirt, vestcoat, coat, trousers, cloth socks, shoes all at the same time. It is a ludicrous dress.[9]

Although Dharmapala attempted to distance his ideal national dress from the sarong—a dress which probably originated in Indonesia and came to Sri Lanka through the Malays—what he suggested was in fact a more elegant version of the sarong. The white sarong was indeed commonly worn as the formal dress. The novelist Martin Wickramasinghe has described how as a child in the late nineteenth century he wore a white sarong to go to temple.[10] The dress Dharmapala defined as the national dress was selected precisely with the rural constituency in mind. There would be change, but not a sizeable change in the dress of the farmer. What changed was the pride attached to the dress that was worn.

In the early twenties there were frequent instances of the national dress being worn in official contexts such as the school or the workplace. But at this stage these experiments were severely dealt with. When some students of Trinity College, Kandy went to school wearing national dress, Reverend A.J. Frazer, the warden of the college, made them stand on benches and ridiculed them in front of the whole school.[11] The principal of the Buddhist School Ananda College, Kularatne successfully introduced the national costume in his school. It was reported that a number of government officials, including Sir William Manning praised him for doing so, thus displaying the British tendency to admire things of the past, even if this past was an imagined one. A lawyer's attempt to wear the national dress to court was turned down.[12] It appeared that the national dress was acceptable to the British insofar as it remained within the confines of native social interaction.

The Arya Sinhala Dress for Women

15

The movement, which invented a national dress for men, looked back to the past to suggest a suitable dress for women. Little was known about the clothes worn in pre-colonial times. It is generally believed that in medieval times women's dress was a cloth wrapped round the hip leaving the body bare from the waist upwards. By the fourteenth and fifteenth centuries an upper garment was worn when going out. This stage of the cloth, worn with a separate garment covering the breasts, thrown over the shoulders evolved into the shawl and breastband. The pre-colonial attire, the Aryan dress as it was later called, according to a Sinhala poem of the fifteenth century, was thus a long cloth wrapped around the body and folded thickest at the waist. One end was drawn up and allowed to fall in pleats over the portion that served as the waistband.

The costume of the Sinhalese women before the arrival of the Portuguese, was abandoned in the Low-Country as a result of the widespread adoption of Christianity and the free social intercourse which existed between the Portuguese and the Sinhalese of the upper classes. The great majority of women on the coastal belt took to the Portuguese long sleeved jacket rounded at the back and in front with a V neck line. This style of jacket was called the *kabakuruththuwa* and was only worn by women of the Karava caste (an intermediary caste traditionally associated with fishing). Areas where there was most contact between the natives and the newcomers from Europe were the harbours and military centres.

In the mid-seventeenth century, under the influence of the puritanical Dutch, lace collars, frills, cuffs and hemlines began to be freely used. Lace-making was introduced as a cottage industry.[13] The influence of the later Nayakkar dynasty on the Kandyan throne led to a consequent modification in dress in the Kandyan provinces with the adoption of the *osariya* style of saree by Kandyan upper-class women.[14] In 1921 the dress of the Low-Country Sinhalese woman of the poorer class consisted of

> a bright coloured camboy and a white linen bodice or blouse with a round neck and long sleeves, and sometimes a coloured shawl draped around the shoulders ... A high-caste woman always affects a white bodice and considers it derogatory to be seen in a coloured one as it is sometimes worn by a low-caste woman.[15]

In the Kandyan areas women continued wearing the osariya. Although the early nationalists were not politically motivated when they attempted to gel the features of an ideal national dress for women, the osariya or what resembled it— the 'Aryan dress', their choice was nevertheless informed by a rejection of hybridity. The Low-Country women by adopting so many European styles had, in the view of the reformists, renounced their nation.

In the nationalist ideology of the late nineteenth century and beginning of the twentieth century, the woman had a role to play but it was different from the man's. Her dress too would have to be reformed, but even the reformed dress was not invested with the same symbolic meaning contained in the concept of national dress. While the male national dress conjured political belonging, female dress functioned on a different plane.

The woman embodied the nation, not political institutions or economic riches, but rather the 'carnal pulp and the mystical mana'.[16] The nationalists' interest in propounding a new image of the Sinhalese woman can be explained by the woman's influence over her children and her traditional role as a carer and nurturer in the family. She represented—in their view—the spirit of the house, the family and the home. Reforming the Sinhalese woman and remodelling her meant reforming an entire generation of Sinhalese who would then be open to nationalist ideas and hostile to western rule. At the core of this construction of an ideal woman was the notion of authenticity. The Sinhalese press of the day contained many letters to the editor which reveal the wide interest which was taken in defining the contours of the ideal Sinhalese woman. Foreign customs, it was felt, had to be discarded by her.

> It is a great tragedy that many of our sisters who have become slaves to western civilisation seem to have discarded our ancient customs and manners.[17]

There was also a definite puritan streak in this 'return' to Victorian codes of conduct. Demure in attitude, the Sinhalese woman was expected to speak softly, keep her hair long and avoid any form of clothing, especially short dresses, which could arouse bad passion in men. Clothing had to be modest and decent. Women were not encouraged to expose their navel or ankles. They were expected to shed all garments of foreign origin from brassieres (believed by some to be damaging the breasts of young women) to long skirts, socks, shoes and hats.[18] The saree which was considered an adequate dress for the Sinhalese woman, was promoted by lay preachers throughout the country as the true Sinhalese dress. The saree was a morally acceptable dress: it covered the entire body. Dharmapala's recommendations on 'how females should conduct themselves' were quite clear in that respect.

> A proper blouse should cover the breast, stomach and back completely. A cloth ten *riyans* long should be worn as the osariya or saree.[19]

One reason for the choice of the osariya as the national dress was its Kandyan origin. While the Low-Country was subjected to a spectrum of cultural influences, the Kandyan kingdom had, in the view of the reformists, through its historical insulation, protected its purity. The osariya was seen not only as the 'moral dress' but also as the authentic, unspoiled and 'pure' dress of the Sinhalese.

It is difficult to assess the impact Dharmapala and his fellow-travellers had upon the masses through widely distributed printed pamphlets. But his ideas were not unique in the intellectual stage of the period. Dress reform was a favourite topic of discussion just as were fallen morals and how a woman ought to behave. The national dress constituted an important component of the symbolic fetishes of the nationalist ideology.

The Uniform of Rebellion

Men's national dress became a political issue with the democratisation of politics and the beginning of electoral politics. The enactment of the Donoughmore Constitution in 1931, which abolished communal representation and instituted universal suffrage, initiated a re-conquest of political power by the Sinhalese majority. This re-conquest took many forms. It was a positive operation since it was destined to bring back self-esteem to the people after four hundred years of colonial domination and acculturation. It was also a negative operation, for exorcising the colonial past meant bringing down specific groups which had benefited from it.

I wish to make a simple plea
against the inconsistency
Of those who hastily divest
Them of the garments of the West
For it is true that now and then
You stop to use a fountain pen?
How neat appears the lawyer's brief
Deep scratched upon the ola-leaf?
When sudden fails the light of day
Please light your lamp the Veddah way
And rub a firestick in the dark
Until you get a little spark
Don't think to use a motor car
A hackery is fitter far
If you must travel in the rain
You should not use a railway train
For longer trips a bullock bandy
Though somewhat slow is very handy
When council meets at half-past-two
I'll tell you what you ought to do
Just time your journey by the sun
And if you're there by half-past-one
You'll only have an hour to wait.
That's far better than being late.
When at Queen's House you're asked to dine,
Refuse to taste the foreign wine.
And smilingly say to everybody,
The only drink for me is toddy.
This ends my simple little plea
Against such inconsistency.
For this is very plain to see.
You do it to attract the eyes.
You'd not be noticed otherwise. [20]

Dressing the Political Body

In Sri Lanka, as in India under British rule, wearing a national dress was first and foremost a form of political rebellion against the indignity of having been compulsorily reclothed by a conquering power. It can be seen as a displacement of economic, political and cultural issues. Gandhi redefined normality in dress by wearing a loincloth to meet and negotiate with the British Viceroy Churchill, whose sense of sartorial respectability was offended, called him a 'half-naked fakir' and referred to his dress as 'nauseating' and 'humiliating'.[21] Gandhi had, since the First Non-cooperation Movement of 1920–21, elaborated a political idiom distinct from the British idiom which had until then set the terms of discourse of the early nationalist movement. The Indian National Congress in its incipient form was organised on the same motif as a British political association: it followed the age-old rules of association in its acceptance of notions such as a President, an executive committee, a quorum and, until the 1920s used mainly the petition as a form of protest. As Cohn has subtly shown, Gandhi's contributions to the nationalist movement were concerned with the creation and representation of new codes of conduct based on a radically different theory of authority. By wearing homespun, simple peasant clothes instead of the native costumes decreed by the imperial rulers, by meeting at communal prayer meetings instead of political rallies, and by adopting the Indian pilgrimage and padayatra as new political rituals, Gandhi's followers were in fact creating a new political idiom of resistance.[22]

In Ceylon the religio-cultural movement of the early twentieth century was overshadowed by a moderate and reformist trend spearheaded by the Ceylon National Congress that never evolved from the British idiom in which it was initially anchored. It remained an elitist association of lawyers and professionals which functioned along the colonial rules of political organisation. In Congress deliberations, members were referred to as 'gentlemen'.[23] Could gentlemen wear a national dress? The CNC's encouragement to the national dress movement was not deeply rooted in a full-fledged resistance to British rule. While preaching the benefits of wearing the national dress CNC leaders continued to drink Scotch Whisky in their clubs, accept honours bestowed by the British, and in their political activism, seldom used any other political idiom than that of British colonialism. The uniform of rebellion remained an isolated marking that contested authority and its limited spread to the population as a whole can be explained by the absence of any general idiom contesting British authority. The national dress was an exception in a transfer of power which was essentially characterised by continuity with the colonial state and its emblems. The adoption of the national dress by a few politicians belonging to more radical groups such as the Sinhalese Maha Sabha was not accompanied by significant changes in the political culture of the nationalist movement.

The symposium of views on dress reform in the *Ceylon Daily News* in 1931 points towards two main concerns: the renouncement of western clothes and the adoption of a true (authentic) dress for the Ceylonese man and woman. In 1931 politicians took the lead. C.W. Kannangara, Sir H. de Mel and W.A. de Silva were among the first to adopt the cloth on public occasions.[24] S.W.R.D. Bandaranaike is perhaps more renowned for wearing the cloth to the State Council and Governor's dinners as he informed the press of his dress before such occasions. For a man who wore court dress as a child and a bowler hat during his years at Oxford, Bandaranaike's concern with dress reform from the beginning of his career as State Councillor may seem incongruous. In fact dress was just one component of the principles which guided his political agenda of return to Sinhalese Buddhism.

Among those, who in the 1930s articulated concerns about adopting a national dress, there was a general consensus on the adoption of the cloth (sarong) as national dress for men, although peripheral issues like the colour of the cloth was still subject to reservations: was the funereal white necessary? The dress etiquette in courts was also challenged. Indeed gowns and lounge coats were hardly suitable in a tropical climate. The adoption of the cloth in schools as a uniform for school children was also suggested on occasions.[25] The national dress movement was not limited to politicians. Indeed, the clerical staff of the department of Post and Telecommunication decided to reorganise the office dress as a means of cutting down costs by wearing the national dress at office. It was estimated that the cost of the dress manufactured in local fabric—white cloth, long sleeved white banian and the shawl —would amount to less than Rs 3 per unit. At a meeting held at the main post office or GPO, over a hundred clerks of the Post and Telecommunication department promised to attend office clad in the national costume. In this group it is interesting to note that there were 60 Sinhalese and 62 Tamils. Approval was obtained from the head of the department.[26]

In the decades that followed, economic reasons led to the adoption of a national dress by the poorer classes; amongst the upper classes, eager to demonstrate their distance from an alien culture, it was a way of defying colonial authorities. Western dress was then an expression of 'the surrender of culture and bankruptcy in all the creative life of the people'. The solution proposed by a young radical Sinhalese was simple: 'Correction can only be applied in reorganising the social life at the top of society. In short we must change our dress'.[27] The more conservative Ceylon National Congress demonstrated its mitigated concern for dress reform by organising a dress parade in 1941. All competitors agreed that the cloth was the most suitable national dress but differences arose with regard to the upper garment. The winner, chosen by an impressive panel of judges—G.C.S. Corea, H.W. Amarasuriya, Dr R. Saravanamuttu, J.R. Jayewardene and M.D.A. Wijesinghe—was described in these terms:

> He wore a cloth and shirt in the form of a tunic falling just above the knees. The 'tails' of the shirt were elegantly stitched up with pockets on either side. The shirt was taken in at the waist so as to give it a comfortable fit.[28]

One would have to wait for the 1950s and S.W.R.D. Bandaranaike's term of office for a counter-elite to activate the national dress issue. In 1956, the Prime Minister as well as his cabinet of thirteen who he presented to the Governor General Sir Oliver Goonetileke, were dressed in cloth and banian,[29] thus distancing themselves symbolically from the westernised political elite of the previous government.

In countries like Swaziland where one African group was numerically as well as politically dominant, traditional leaders were able to reinforce traditional clothing as a symbol of national identity. In countries with competing ethnic groups separate ethnic costumes were symbolically divisive and a new national costume was designed such as in Tanzania, where, in 1968, the Government banned the wearing of the *hangd*, the traditional red-ochre dyed *toga* of the Barabaig and replaced it with shirts and shorts.[30]

22

While Ceylon fell into the first category, its leaders did not try to impose the Kandyan costume on all, but rather created a national dress which resembled the dress of the common man whether Sinhala, Tamil or Muslim. Ethnic groups could show their distinctiveness by wearing additional adornment such as a turban for Tamils or a fez for the Muslims. In effect the created national dress became an expression of majoritarian culture, i.e. of the Sinhalese, while minority leaders often preferred wearing the western coat and trousers at formal occasions. Unlike their Indian counterparts, the Sinhala literati were not totally successful in their attempt to create a uniform of rebellion. In the decades that followed, they found themselves in an increasing variety of sartorially perplexing situations.

Choosing a Day

In India, a few months before Ceylon obtained independence, Jawaharlal Nehru clad in a sherwani had heralded the beginning of the new dominion. Nehru, who had the qualities of a visionary, was not oblivious to the fact that clothing was an important symbol through which an Indian polity would come to be imagined. Few people remember however that the sherwani is a buttoned frock-coat that was an adaptation of some faction in the Mughal court to European fashions in an attempt to establish alliances with the Europeans. Rather than signifying distance from the West it denoted a critical shift towards western dress.

National day in India was selected because it linked the past and the present, because it was embedded in the history of struggle. Since 1930, the national flag was hoisted in the morning followed by a march to a public meeting where Congress delegates and audience were solemnly to repeat the words of the *purna swaraj* or Independence Day pledge. The pledge which had been drafted by Gandhi and Nehru defined the freedom Congress had now adopted as its primary objective.

Our calendar tells us today that India's Republic Day is on 26 January. The date was chosen because 26 January had been an essential part of the immediate past of the liberation struggle. Nehru made the connection clear in his message to the nation on the inauguration of the Republic:

> The day links up the past with the present, and this present is seen to grow out of the past. Twenty years ago we took the first pledge of independence. During these twenty years we have known struggle and conflict and failure and achievement. Yet undoubtedly, 26 January 1950 is a day of high significance for India and the Indian people.[31]

India became a Republic on 26 January 1950. This date then became Republic Day and the nation's major event for celebration. The other date—15 August remained as Independence Day and confusion between naming the two occasions disappeared. Republic Day on 26 January became the day for national celebration rather than the one on which India had fortuitously become independent. There were too many painful memories surrounding 15 August: the traumas of partition, the communal holocaust and the millions of refugees. Sardar Patel summarised it in his 1950 Republic Day message:

> ... Although we obtained independence on August 15, 1947, it was not complete in the sense of the pledge that we took. Today, by the grace of God, that pledge has been completely fulfilled.[32]

The Indian national days complemented one another, they both made sense in the collective consciousness of the people.

By comparison, 4 February was an insignificant designate for Sri Lanka's commemoration as a nation. Why was it chosen when there were other choices available? In 1915 the Centenary of the Kandyan Convention was celebrated on 30 March. A year earlier, a National Day was celebrated on 13 April, the traditional Sinhalese and Hindu New Year day, as an essentially Sinhalese National Day where only Sinhalese were invited. The celebrations were organised by the Sinhalese Young Men's Association. These two dates had more, if not profound significance for the people of the island.[33]

Dates can function as foundation myths. When in 1880 the Republican deputies were called to adopt a glorious date as France's national day of festivity they had a choice, a political choice to make between different moments of the Revolution—the bourgeois revolution of 1789, or the democratic revolution of 1792. The choice of 14 July, the day of the capture of the Bastille, meant the Republic would respect and honour the heritage of the democratic Revolution. The date 14 July constituted for those who initiated it, an embodiment of republican values and an incarnation of the Republic through popular acts and spectacles. These values could only be internalised by the individual through a collective celebration which had to be organised in a proper fashion.[34]

The choice of the national day reveals something of the nationalism that glorifies it. For instance National Day in Ghana was not the day the country achieved independence but the birthday of its president Nkrumah, thus revealing that the new national state rested chiefly on a personality. So Ghana's national day lasted only as long as he did. In South Vietnam the official national day is the anniversary of the murder of President Diem.[35] This choice suggested the spirit of revanchism and the lack of forgiveness in the new nation state. It also eulogised violence.

In Ceylon, the national day symbolised nothing of the past of the state. For many people it signified little. But others, through haphazard collective acts, invested it with a new meaning, a meaning which went back to the myths of foundation of the Sinhalese and to memories of anti-colonial struggle.

Unofficial Memories

While D.S. Senanayake was celebrating in his top hat and tails, various people were living the day in different ways. Some people remembered, but what they remembered resembled more present-day celebrations than anything connected with an anti-colonial struggle.

In schools and institutions, children, dressed in osariya (half saree) or young adults dressed in white sarees, offered flowers and lit oil lamps. The Principal addressed the children and explained the significance of Independence. Mrs Meegama, who was then a child of twelve in Kandy, remembers large processions of people hoisting Lion Flags and singing about Sri Lanka. 'Some people were holding large pictures and parading on the streets'.[36] In her family home, Mrs P. Magalage remembers getting milk-rice, cake and bananas in the morning and in the evening going to the temple with her parents and grandfather. At school there were celebrations such as waving the Lion Flag and singing the national anthem before all went to the temple.[37]

Memories differed little in their uniformity. They were atemporal. They had a peculiar official and sanitised quality which seemed to be the product of fifty years of pounding of the drum of nationalism, of an enmeshment of the past and the present where the present had changed everything of the past. These memories revealed nothing of the pain, humiliations and angers which might have come with growing up under colonial rule. If these feelings were absent their absence too was outside memory. The memories of those questioned had no place for the unconscious or for the political. Strangely no one spoke of colonialism or the end of foreign rule. It was a time of absence of mind, a time to rejoice rather than reflect.

Official celebrations were sometimes reshaped by the personality of its organisers. This reflected divergent perceptions on nationalism and the conspicuous absence of unity of purpose even in the celebrations at an official level. Each one lived it as a personal experience and the official stance was often subverted. Distinct people had their own distinct forms of consciousness and acted upon the world in their own terms. In Negombo the emphasis was on social service rather than sumptuous celebrations. The Lion Flag was hoisted and free meals were distributed to the poor. In the afternoon, several thousands of school children rallied opposite the old Dutch Fort. Before proceedings started, the Chairman of the Negombo Urban Council dressed in national costume, white cloth and shawl, requested those assembled to observe a minute of silence as a mark of respect for Mahatma Gandhi.[38] By honouring the Indian nationalist leader instead of any sons of the soil, any Ceylonese national hero, the Chairman of the Negombo UC was making a clear and uncompromising political statement. Ceylon had no real nationalist fighter, no leader of the masses who united or attempted to unite classes, castes and religions of the calibre of Mahatma Gandhi.

But the fact that the UC Chairman had sufficient freedom of mind to celebrate independence as he understood it, according to his own ideals and hopes, reflected that at least independence had been achieved in a small way.

There were people of this predominantly Catholic Negombo who celebrated independence in yet another way. After the mass at St Mary's Church, one of the largest churches in Ceylon, Boy Scouts and Girl Guides formed a guard of honour in front of the Church and a large number of school children sang the national anthem, the music of which was composed by Rabindranath Tagore. The people then assembled round the very spot where, according to popular tradition, in 1815, the last King of Kandy, Sri Wickrama Rajasinghe, took shelter while being led in captivity to Colombo and exiled to Mauritius.

On Independence Day, a Kandyan king of southern Indian descent who had adopted the Buddhist faith, was celebrated as a hero in a coastal southern town by the Catholic community. It was indeed a strange choice to celebrate the last king of Kandy as the symbol of a free nation.[39] Sri Wickrama Rajasinghe was the last of the Nayakkar dynasty to rule Kandy. The Nayakkars were a Telugu family originally from Madurai. They had later moved to the coast and were little better than petty chiefs. However both Wimaladharmasuriya II and Narendrasinha obtained their queens from this group. But they were 'alien in ethnicity, language, religion and their aspects of culture'. Sri Wickrama Rajasinghe ascended the throne in 1798 and was considered a just ruler at first. Later, however, he seems to have turned into a true tyrant extracting heavy taxes, executing his one-time ministers and members of the *sasana* (Buddhist clergy). The resentment that built up against him was tinged with racialist overtones. He was on some occasions branded as a 'heretical Tamil'.[40]

27

One wonders at the reasons which led a Low-Country coastal village to celebrate on independence day a 'foreign' king of the Kandyan kingdom reputed for his tyranny. One is possibly ignorance. Perhaps the feats of the Nayakkars were not known to the modern Ceylonese who had learnt in school more about the history of Britain than the history of their own land. Perhaps it was simply the dearth of national heroes which made the people of Negombo choose such an unlikely person to celebrate. After Sri Wickrama possibly no 'historical figure' had ever set foot in Negombo.

Individuals lived independence in very special and personal ways. On Independence Day, Charles Andrew Perera Warnakula Jayasuriya of Kalamulla decided 'as a mark of rejoicing at the regaining of Independence by Ceylon', to 'drop all my foreign names and take on 'appropriate Sinhalese names: His new name was Chandrasekera Ananda Prasanna Warnakula Jayasuriya.[41]

Black Flags

The *Lankadipa* reported that some black flags were displayed at Nathatdiya as a protest against the 800,000 rupees allegedly spent on the celebrations.[42] The Left newspaper *Nidahasa* recalls that students were caned by their teacher for refusing to participate in the Independence Day festivities or bringing flags to schools.[43]

The anti-independence protests were, it seems, limited to the Left movements who argued that Ceylon was not really independent and that there was nothing worth celebrating.

This was perhaps why some popular celebrations looked back to myths rather than to an uneventful nationalist history. While celebrations organised by the state did not refer back to any past—nationalist, colonial or precolonial—celebrations outside the spectrum of the state sometimes displayed another colour. In some schools, plays based on mythic histories were enacted to celebrate independence day. One of these was the Rama and Sita legend. Through this act it was the mythic past which was invoked to celebrate the caesura from British rule. These foundation myths of the Sinhalas, which had been rekindled by the literati of the early twentieth century through the serialisation in newspapers, the plays and novels of John de Silva and Piyadasa Sirisena were invested with a new life.

The popular celebrations which referred to a pre-Aryan colonisation of Ceylon, contemporaneous with the original Aryan colonisation of southern India, suggested a lengthy history of Ceylon as a country/state if not as a sovereign nation-state. The myth of Ravana was part of the imaginary of the people of the island. The story goes that Ravana, King of Lanka, hearing of the beauty of Sita, the wife of Rama (then in exile) abducted and brought her to Lanka. Rama having allied himself with the non-Aryan races of southern India, crossed over to Lanka, gave battle to Ravana, defeated him and recovered Sita. This story was commonly known in the late nineteenth and early twentieth century. The *Lak Mini Kirula*, an early Sinhala newspaper, carried in a 1881 issue, the first part of the serialised history of Lanka. It was claimed that Lanka was 'a powerful kingdom even prior to the advent of Vijaya' and that the mythical ruler Ravana had ruled the island in about 2837 B.C. with the assistance of a council of ten.[44] The precision of the dates supports Barthes's contention that myth as 'depoliticised speech' *(parole)* does not deny things, that its function is on the contrary to speak about things simply. It purifies them and founds them in nature and eternity, gives them a clarity which is not that of the explanation but of the statement.[45] Later publications too reiterated the Ravana myth:

> Prior to the landing of Vijaya, however, in the sixth century before Christ—from which date the written history of Ceylon

28

begins—it is now conceded that the island was peopled by advanced races and that its history as a civilised country dates many centuries from Vijaya's occupation:[46]

Why was Ravana King of Lanka, who after all had lost to the virtuous Rama, celebrated on Independence Day? If the myth functioned as analogy it would suggest that the British, like Rama, were leaving but taking with them as the prize possession of Lanka, Sita. Sita who symbolised the honour of the Sinhalese was taken away. All that was left was the dejected Ravana.

29

Curiously there were only a few reported occurrences of the Vijayan myth being re-enacted in popular manifestations inspite of the role of the indigenous press, and the two newly emerging genres of the theatre and the novel that were crucial in the popularising of stories described in the Mahavamsa.[47] According to Sinhala-Buddhist tradition, fashioned largely by the *Vamsa* literature, Sri Lanka is the *Dharmadvipa* (the island of the faith) consecrated by the Buddha himself as the land in which his teachings would flourish.[48] The *Mahavamsa*, a sixth-century court chronicle states that on the very day of the Buddha's death, Vijaya—the founder of the Sinhala race —landed in Sri Lanka, as if to bear witness to the Buddha's prediction.[49] The *Mahavamsa* as a written text was valued more by nationalists than folktales and oral culture and the revivalist leaders, in their search for ethnically and energising themes from the community's historical tradition, found a most satisfying solution in the belief of Aryan origins in northern India. Prince Vijaya was believed to have come from north India, the *Aryavarta* as it was called in Sanskrit texts.

The Sinhalese people were the repository and the creators of these myths and histories but the official celebrations did not relate to either Vijaya, Ravana or any other folk memories. Was it a conscious decision that was taken in order to project a secular image to which all communities would relate? The mythical past of the Sinhalese and its multifaceted experiences were drawn upon by the state only in a few haphazard occurrences: Independence was chiefly enacted as an imperial ceremony.

Independence: The Ultimate Imperial Ceremony

The events and celebrations of transfer of power show that continuities between colonial rule and the post-colonial state prevailed in the minds of the statesmen of the day.

Parade

The Transfer-of-power ceremony from British to Ceylonese hands was very much an imperial ceremony on the lines of the ceremonies that took place to mark the arrival and departure of governors to and from their colonies. By wearing his bowler hat and suit, D.S. Senanayake was a radical contrast to his nationalist brothers across the Palk straits. The paradox of dress symbolism was indeed perfectly exposed in the drama of nationalism in India: if the British dressed up in splendid uniforms to establish and maintain authority over the Indians, the nationalists dressed down to grasp back the power that had been wrested from them. Hence Gandhi's loin cloth. Imperial ceremonies were an occasion for British rule to display before the eyes of the world and its native subjects that it was still alive.

The independence ceremony was not different from others except that it was the ultimate one. Imperial ceremonies reached their height in Curzon's India, but such ceremonies were later also seen in Africa and the Pacific. Kirk-Greens has described the dress of the governor of a colony:

> He was entitled to wear either a white uniform with white and red plumes in his colonial helmet or, in cooler climates, a dark blue uniform with a cocked hat and white plumes. Gold and silver gorgets, epaulettes, buttons, and frogging and an elaborately decorated sword completed the uniform.[50]

The triumphant entry of Sir Bernard Bourdillon to the Nigerian scene in 1935 has been described thus:

> On the morning of his arrival we all went down to the customs wharf, the men in white uniforms and the ladies superb in their best. ... The Regiment mounted one of its im-

maculate Guards of Honour and the band played on a flank. The invited guests sat uncomfortably in their finery on hard chairs, carefully arranged in the order in which they had to be presented. The guns (brought specially from Zaria) fired their slow salute from across the water. ... Then the tall figure of Sir Bernard came down the companion way in his blue uniform and plumes, with his dazzling wife.[51]

The Independence Day celebrations in Ceylon resembled an imperial fete with a few of the artifices of the nation state: national anthem and national flag. National dress was interestingly absent. Its resemblance to the Jubilee celebrations of Queen Victoria which occurred in the late nineteenth century is striking. John Ferguson has left a fascinating account of the celebrations that started with a military review on Galle Face Green Esplanade which included volunteers marching and *feu de joie*. On that day, services were held in all places of worship. A large number of poor people in towns and villages were fed, each getting a measure of rice and five cents (one penny) or a piece of calico. This act of charity was followed by great celebrations at Galle Face Esplanade where fifteen to twenty *pandals* were erected. They were decorated with loops of plantain and coconut leaf, green moss and fern, yellow *olas*. Approximately 25,000 people were present to hear the Governor read the 'Record of the chief events of the fifty years'. The Royal Standard was hoisted and a salute of fifty guns was heard. The Royal Anthem was sung. A procession of two thousand people followed including 27 Buddhist monks and Arabi Pasha, (the leader of the abortive Egyptian uprising of 1882, exiled in Ceylon between 1883 and 1901).

This was the script of the celebrations which to a large extent was going to be followed only with minor modifications in 1948. The fact that in one case a Queen of a foreign land was being celebrated for her reign of fifty years, and on the other, this same land was gaining independence from a foreign land, did not lead to many changes: the same ingredients were there, hoisting of flag, military parade, religious ceremonies, speeches, acts of charity.[52]

As Independence Day came near, the buntings went up in the streets, and soon the guests began to pour in from the Commonwealth and other foreign countries as well as from the United Kingdom itself. The British government was represented officially by the Minister of State for Colonial Affairs. The Duke of Gloucester would represent the Sovereign and inaugurate Ceylon's new status.

The chief event of February was the swearing in of Sir Henry Monck Mason Moore as the first Governor-General of the dominion of Ceylon at a solemn but brief ceremony at Queens House in the morning. The Governor-General had his oaths administered to him by the Chief Justice, Sir John Howard in the presence of the cabinet ministers and the parliamentary Under-Secretary to the British Commonwealth Relations Office, Mr Patrick Gordon Walker.

The Prime Minister D.S. Senanayake was the first to congratulate the new Governor-General after the latter's swearing-in. In the evening the Governor-General and Lady Moore attended Divine Service at the Wolfendhal Church where the preacher was the assistant Bishop of Colombo. They drove to church in the new Rolls Royce which was to be used by the Duke of Gloucester during his stay in Ceylon.[53]

In Colombo, at the stroke of the auspicious moment, a *Day Perahera* set off from the Punchikawatte Temple; the Chief Elephant in the procession carried a Lion Flag. The Perahera then proceeded along Darley Road and reached the Eye Hospital Junction where 132 *bhikkus* from the Jayawardenapura monastery, Kotte, joined the procession. The significance of bhikkus from this monastery was that this monastery had been the repository of the sacred Tooth Relic, prior to its removal to the Dalada Maligawa.

The procession then went along Alexandra Place up to the foot of the F.R. Senanayake statue. To the accompaniment of the firing of 132 detonators and the chanting of *pirith*, five Lion Flags were hoisted by the Prime Minster, Mr D.S. Senanayake, the Minister of Home Affairs and Rural Reconstruction, Sir Oliver Goonetilake, the Minister of Finance, Mr J.R. Jayawardena, and a few others.[54]

As part of the amnesty granted for independence, 1,186 prisoners were released.[55]

Religious Fetes

The Methodist Church united with other Protestant churches in Galle in a special thanksgiving to be held at the Dutch Reformed Church. But the imperial fete was neither the theatre of a general religious reconciliation nor did it grow into an occasion for the unification of men and women who shared the common ideal of freedom. In this sense it offered a sharp contrast with other national celebrations. In France for instance, through the different components of the fete on the public roads (inauguration of statues, processions, commemorations of different sorts, torchlight retreats) the French republic was able to take away from the Catholic Church the near exclusive control of the social space and of the festive and ludic domains that it exerted since 1815—a transfer of sacrality from the religious to the secular, the civic and the profane.

33

The difference in Ceylon was that the religious entered the domain of the fete, and the nation was celebrated differently by each of its religious groups: in churches for Christians, in mosques for Muslims, in temples for Buddhists.

Harbour, Zoo, Museum

The Harbour, the Zoo and the Museum were the sites of large celebrations. The Colombo Harbour symbolised the commercial power of Ceylon built up by colonialism. Thousands flocked to Colombo on the night of 4 February to witness the water fete in the Harbour and the illuminations in other parts of the city. According to newspaper reports, not since the return of the Regalia of the King of Kandy had such a crowd been seen in the city. The waterfront area presented a sea of heads from the breakwater to Mutwal. People had climbed cranes and the roofs of waterhouses and other vantage places to get a good view. All ships, tugs and barges were lit up and the harbour presented a blaze of colour. Some had bought and wore their Independence badge which represented the Lion, the mythic ancestor of the Sinhalese.[56]

Admiral Sir Arthur Palliser, the Commander-in-Chief of the East Indies Squadron, switched on the illuminated word *nidahasa* (freedom) set high up on the jib of the pontoon named *Jumbo*. Kandyan dances by Ceylon's finest exponents of the art were described as 'the most interesting feature of the night's entertainment'.

It was reported that the floating stage was too far from the audience and the music by the marines of H.M.S. Norfolk was not heard by many. Illuminated boats with multi-coloured lights skimming the placid waters, with illuminated cranes in the distance, made a picturesque scene. A coloured water-jet display and fireworks added to the entertainment.[57]

34

The Zoo and the Museum were part of a new apparatus of representation which had contributed in the colonial period to constructing the colonial master's other. Museums were first created in Europe as monuments designed to retain the collective memory of nations. National Archives were opened in France after the Revolution, and in 1838, Britain organised a Public Records Office. From the end of the eighteenth century onwards, national museums and public libraries opened their doors to the public. The purpose was quite clearly to manufacture national identity and consolidate the bases of the nation.[58] Colonialism, however, transformed the function of the museum: museums now organised the representation of the world, the world as an 'exhibit'. Museums in Europe with their increased collections of oriental artefacts, became not only the repository of the strange, but the site where these objects were ordered under glass in a rational manner—the order of evolution. The Zoo too was a product of nineteenth-century colonial penetration of the Orient and the interest of European people in strange species. The Colombo Zoo, however, was never used by colonisers to vindicate racial superiority of the white race. This was not the case in the New York Bronx Zoo where at the beginning of the century, a pygmy from the Congo had been displayed in the same cage as an orangutang.[59]

The Colombo Museum had been established in the 1870s by Sir William Gregory, the Governor of the island. In his speech to the Legislative Council he explicitly conveyed what were, in his view, the aims of a museum. The purpose of the Colombo Museum was articulated as two-fold—amusement at the sight of objects of wonderment, and education.[60] On

Independence Day, while on the streets an imperial fete was staged, inside the boundaries and the walls of the austere white building graced with the presence of Boehm's statue of Governor Gregory, the people of the land were learning about themselves by looking into glass cages. Large crowds visited the Museum, while the record number of 135,600 visited the Dehiwela Zoo on Independence Day. There were 30,000 in the zoo at a time and the record attendance amounted to 260 a minute.[61] The Zoo and the Museum were emblematic colonial institutions which had been uncritically coopted by the new nation state.

History as Exhibit

An exhibition of objects of special historical and cultural interest was held at the museum. The exhibition was opened by the Minister of Education, Mr E.A. Nugawela, thus exemplifying the state's understanding of the museum as a space of learning. The idiom introduced by the Europeans when they created the Museum was unproblematically adopted by the nationalists. Modes of representation—glass cages, modes of explanation—vignette-like labels summarising the historical relevance of an object, modes of ordering—chronological and evolutionary, modes of periodising—according to the dynasties and reigns of kings, showed a continuity between colonial and post-colonial cultural forms.

Among the historical exhibits were collection of seals and signatures of Sinhalese kings: among them Bhuvaneka Bahu, Don Juan Dharmapala, Parakramabahu VI, Vijaya VII of Kotte, Vickramabahu and Senarat of Kandy and Mayadunne of Sitawaka. The choice of kings was revealing: each kingdom was represented from the Christian Don Juan to the Buddhist Mayadunne. The absence of any king of Tamil descent from the kingdom of Jaffna was suggestive of the creating of an identity which was composite, but resolutely selective. If Tamil political power was left in a shadow, Tamil culture was very much present. Objects of art and culture on exhibition included a collection of Hindu bronzes such as the famous Nataraja figure, Saiva saints, Sundaramurti and

Mannikakavanayar. The Buddhist bronzes included two masterpieces of Indian art, the Badulla sedent Buddha and the Anuradhapura Trivaka Maitreya Bodhisattva.

The archaeological department lent a collection of estampages of important lithic inscription. They were exhibited with a chart showing the gradual development of the Sinhalese scripts during the last 2,000 years. Provincial flags were displayed. A special case of important palm leaf manuscripts exhibits the copy of Sulu Vaga, the oldest known manuscript in the museum, an illuminated copy of *Vessantara Jataka*, and specimens of richly carved silver covers of manuscripts. These objects, and many others that were exhibited at the Colombo Museum, constituted for the new nation-state the national heritage which it would cherish and protect. The inclusion of Veddah dances in the programme of celebrations in some districts of the North Central Province such as Mannampitiya showed a desire to exhibit the curious, the bizarre and the different. The museumising of certain ethnic groups at the margins of the nation began with this process, which equated tradition with curiosity.[62]

Other Imperial Fetes: Africa

Ten years later when Ghana gained independence, one of the first acts of the Duchess of Kent, who represented the Empire, was to open the Ghana Museum which housed the collection begun by the University College in 1951. She also attended a regatta which was held in the harbour. But unlike in Ceylon, memories of colonial violence were not subdued. Just after dark, the Duchess of Kent opened the Independence Monument erected near the spot where in 1948 members of the ex-servicemen's union were shot when marching to Christianborg Castle to present a petition to the Governor. On the inner wall of the monument a commemorative tablet unveiled by the Duchess read:

Ghana's Independence, 6 March 1957. Let this monument hold sacred in your memory the liberty and freedom of Ghana: the liberty and freedom which by our struggle and sacrifice the people of Ghana have this day regained. May this independence be preserved and held sacred for all time.

Dr Nkrumah, the Prime Minister, the Governor and the Duchess then watched a display of fireworks from the top of the monument.[63]

Three years later when Nigeria became independent, the same ingredients of the imperial ceremony were present with a few changes and additions. Britain surrendered sovereignty in the presence of Princess Alexandra as representative of the Queen. A spectacular searchlight tattoo took place at the Lagos race-course, watched by 40,000 people in which the Nigerian Army, Navy and Police took part. There was also a realistic mock battle between armoured cars and a 25-pounder gun representing an anti-tank gun. The new green and white flag of Nigeria was hoisted in place of the Union Jack on a floodlit flagpole at the Lagos race-course. A final salute was given to the Union Jack by a guard of honour of Nigerian, Ghanian and Rhodesian–Nyasaland troops, while 'God Save the Queen' was sung in the full. Immediately afterwards the guard of honour gave a first formal public salute to the flag of independent Nigeria and all three verses of the new Nigerian National Anthem were sung in full. At midnight, ships in the harbour sounded their sirens and crowds on the waterfront and in the streets started cheering and dancing in the streets. A display of fireworks followed the official flag-raising.

National flag, national anthem, national army were the symbolic creations, the new emblems of the independent state. The rejoicing was more spontaneous than in Ceylon where a certain amount of self-reflection, largely promoted by the state, had led people to flock to the museum. The harbour remained the privileged site of celebration in both new states, while fireworks spoke a universal language.[64] There is no account of the dress of the Nigerians to whom power was transmitted, this lets one guess that it did not call for a comment and was most likely European formal wear. It was still not time to display one's nativeness. Modernity was the value to be exhibited by the new rulers and the western suit was the epitome of modernity.

In 1963 when Kenya gained its freedom, more concessions were made to native culture although the symbols of the nation state—flag, national song—were central.

> For three hours before the moment of independence arrived, the crowd was entertained with tribal dancing and a parade. The ceremony was attended by 25 Mau Mau 'generals' immaculate in British-style officers' uniform, with Kenyatta medallions as hat badges.[65]

This description is reminiscent of the way in which the Veddahs were exhibited in the Independence Day celebration on the North Western Province in Ceylon. Native culture in both cases were exhibits which belonged to the realm of the curious and the local. In contrast the generals, who symbolised the power of the new nation state to legitimately coerce, wore modern clothes modelled on their former colonial master's outfits. Traditional clothing had yet to assume significance.

In the late 1960s the context had changed. For the independence ceremony of Swaziland in 1968, the King, the Queen Mother as well as the regiments, the queens and the princesses appeared in full *Incwala* or national costume. This costume varied according to age, sex and status. An adult male would for instance wear a loin-cloth and penis-covering and his body would be decorated with beads of different shape, size and colours, feathers of special birds and skins of selected animals. After political independence, Swazi clothing became the norm at national and international gatherings.[66]

Whether in Africa or in Asia, cultural nationalism was one avenue for the expression of political nationalism. While some leaders emphasised the traditional cultural idiom others copied a British model. A last snapshot of Independence Day in Ceylon speaks more than any explanation.

Independence Day in Negombo, a predominantly Catholic area, began with services in temples, mosques and churches. At St Mary's Church, Grand Street, where a ceremonial High Mass was sung, lawyers attended in their gowns and wigs, officers in uniforms and ladies in dazzling sarees. All this 'added lustre to the decorated church'. Thus Independence Day was a day for dressing up the town and its elites, and it is no accident that the metaphor of dress appears constantly in the descriptions of the festivities.[67]

Although the civil space was tamed by the new state through its state-sponsored celebrations, there was an emptiness characterised by the conspicuous lack of ideological fervour. The illuminated letters of *Nidahas* were only senseless scribbles. The pomp and ostentatious celebration was a desperate bid to evoke memories of historicity justifying a composite civilisation. The unfortunate negating factor was that there was no discernible trend of colonial struggle, which as in India's case could weave the people into a composite whole.

The men who had inherited the mantle of power were still uncertain of what 'national' meant and how the nation should be represented. As a conglomerate of various communities and religions, as the property of westernised elites of different ethnic communities, as the nation of the Sinhalese bearer of the Lion Flag, or as hope for the most deprived people in the country? In doubt, it was deemed suitable to reluctantly promote the white cloth and banian as national dress for the 'others', and wear top hat and tails on formal occasions.

One is tempted today to read new meanings in the text of Independence Day: Hereros in Southern Africa believe that if you wear the clothes of your enemy, the spirit of your enemy is weakened.[68] Could this have been the hidden text of the bowler hat?

NOTES

1. The *Ceylon Daily News*. 26 February 1948.
2. CO 537/692 (Colonial Office), Public Records Office, Kew, U.K.
3. U. R. von Ehrenfels. *The Fabrics of Culture: The Anthropology of Clothing and Adornment*. The Hague Mouton: 1979: 399.
4. N. C. Chaudhuri. *Culture in the Vanity Bag*. Bombay: Jaico: 1976: 58.
5. For more details on the Sinhalese and Tamil social and cultural movements under British colonialism see Kitsiri Malalgoda. *Buddhism in Sinhalese Society (1750–1900): A Study of Religious Revival and Change*. Berkeley and Los Angeles, University of

California Press: 1976, Dagmar Hellmann Rajanayagam. 'Arumuka Navalar: Religious Reformer or National Leader of Eelam'. *Indian Economic and Social History Review* 26. 1989: 235–57.

6. Cited in Phyllis M. Martin. 'Christians and Clothing in French Congo'. (African History Seminar) 28 November 1990. SOAS. Unpublished.

7. A. Guruge (ed.). *Anagarika Dharmapala: Return to Righteousness*. Government Press: Colombo. 1965: 509.

40

8. *Ibid*: 42.

9. *Ibid*.

10. Martin Wickramasinghe. *Upandasita*. Dehiwela: Tisara Publishers. 1961: 44.

11. *The Sinhala Jatiya*. 1 August 1921.

12. *The Sinhala Jatiya*. 11 September 1923.

13. F. Media. 'A Short History of Fashion in Ceylon'. *The Radio Times*. 1972: 3, 12, 20.

14. C.M. Fernando. 'Costume of the Sinhalese Ladies before the Portuguese Period'. *Spolia Zeylanica*. 4. (14 & 15) December 1906: 142.

15. J. B. David. 'National Costumes in Ceylon'. *Times of Ceylon* (Christmas Number) 1921: 24, 27, 44, 47, 50, 51, 55.

16. Simone de Beauvoir. *Le Deuxieme Sexe* (Vol. I). Gallimard, Paris. 1949: 283.

17. *Sarasavi Sanderesa Saha Sinhala Samaja*. 18 January 1924.

18. *Ariya Sinhala Wansaya*. 11 March 1913; *Sinhala Jatiya*. 22 July 1913.

19. A. Guruge (ed.) *Dharmapala Lipi*. Colombo: Government Press. Colombo. 1963: 37.

20. *The Ceylon Daily News*. 10 July 1931. This poem was signed S. Waraj.

21. A. Nandy. *Traditions, Tyranny and Utopias: Essays in the Politics of Awareness*. Delhi: Oxford University Press. 1987: 144.

22. B.S. Cohn. 'Representing Authority in Victorian India'. In E. Hobsbawm and T. Ranger (eds.). *The Invention of Tradition*. Cambridge: Cambridge University Press. 1983: 209

23. See, for instance, Minutes of the Committee Meeting of the CNC of 17 August 1920 in Michael Roberts (ed.). *Documents of the Ceylon National Congress and Nationalist Politics in Ceylon: 1929–1950*, Vol. I. Sri Lanka National Congress and Nationalist Politics in Vol. I. Sri Lanka National Archives, Colombo. 1972: 242.

24. *The Ceylon Daily News.* 7 July1931; 16 July 1931.
25. *The Ceylon Daily News.* 18 July 1931
26. *Dinamina.* 2 July 1931; 4 July 1931.
27. V. Gunasekere. *Young Ceylon.* May 1932.
28. M. Roberts (ed.). *Documents of the Ceylon National Congress and Nationalist Politics in Ceylon: 1929–1950,* Vol. II. Colombo. 1977: 1381.
29. *The Ceylon Daily News.* 13 April 1956.
30. Cited in Hilda Kuper. 'Costume and Identity'. *Comparative Studies in Society and History.* 15, 3, 1973: 359
31. Jim Masselos. 'India's Republic Day: The Other 26 January', *Journal of South Asian Studies:* XIX, Special Issue. 1996: 186–87.
32. *Ibid.*
33. Cited in M. Roberts. 'Problems of Collective Identity in a Multi-Ethnic Society: Sectional Natioinalism *Vs* Ceylonese Nationalism (1900–1940).' In M. Roberts (ed.). *Sri Lanka: Collective Identities Re-visited.* Marga Institute, Colombo: 1945, 451, 459
34. Christian Amalvi. 'Le 14 Juillet. Du Dies Iree a Jour de Fete'. In Pierra Nora (ed.). Les *Lieux de Memoire.* Gallimard: Paris. 1997: 398.
35. Cited in Jim Masselos. 1996: 186.
36. Interview with Mrs Meegama, Panadura, 62 years.
37. Interview with Mrs Magalage, Maharagama, 66 years.
38. *The Times of Ceylon,* 7 February 1948.
39. *Ibid.*
40. K.N.O. Dharmadasa. 'The Sinhala Buddhist Identity and the Nayakkar Dynasty in the Politics of the Kandyan Kingdom: 1739–1815'. In M. Roberts (ed.). *Sri Lanka: Collective Identities Re-visited: Vol. 1:* 79–104.
41. *The Ceylon Daily News,* 5 February 1948.
42. *Lankadipa,* 7 February 1948.
43. *Nidahasa,* 25 February 1948.
44. Cited in K.N.O. Dharmadasa. *The Growth of Sinahlese Nationalism in Sri Lanka,* Michigan: University of Michigan Press. 1992: 120.
45. Roland Barthes. *Mythologies.* Paris: Edition du Seuil, 1957.
46. C.M. Fernando, 'History of Ceylon'. In Arnold Wright (ed.). *Twentieth-Century Impressions of Ceylon: Its History, People, Commerce, Industries and Resources.* London: Lloyd's Greater Britain Publishing Co. 1907: 13.

47. Three figures epitomised these developments: C. Don Bastian (1852–1921), dramatist and journalist; Piyadasa Sirisene (1875–1956), journalist and novelist and John de Silva (1857–1922), dramatist.

48. For an interesting assessment of the Buddhist Chronicles as a dominant site of symbolic production see Steven Kemper. *The Presence of the Past: Chronicles, Politics and Culture in Sinhala Life*. Ithaca: Cornell University Press. 1991.

49. *The Mahavamsa*. Transl. Wilhelm Geiger. Colombo: Government Information Department. 1950.

50. Cited in Helen Callaway. 'Dressing for Dinner in the Bush: Rituals of Self-Definiton and British Imperial Authority'. In R. Barnes and J. Eicher (eds.). *Dress and Gender: Making and Meaning*. Providence, RI/Oxford, Berg. 1993: 241.

51. *Ibid.*

52. John Ferguson. *Ceylon in the Jubilee Year*. A.M.J. Ferguson, Colombo: 1887. 3rd Edn., 171.

53. *The Ceylon Daily News*, 5 February 1948.

54. *Ibid.*

55. *Ibid.*

56. *Ibid.*

57. *Ibid.*

58. Jacques Le Goff. *Histoire et Memoire*. Paris: Gallimard. 1988: 159–60.

59. Adam Rochshild. *King Leopold's Ghost*. New York: Houghton Miffin Company. 1998: 176.

60. Cited in Bethia N. Bell and Heather M. Bell: *H.C.P. Bell: Archaeologist of Ceylon and the Maldives*. Denbigh: Archetype Publications. 1993: 29–30.

61. *The Ceylon Daily News*. 5 February 1948.

62. *The Ceylon Daily News*. 4 February 1958.

63. *The Times of London*. 6 March 1957.

64. *The Times of London*. 1 October 1960.

65. *The Times of London*. 12 December 1963.

66. Hilda Kuper. *Costume and Identity*. 348–67.

67. *The Times of Ceylon*. 7 February 1948.

68. Hildi Hendrickson (ed.). *Clothing and Difference: Embodied Identities in Colonial and Post-Colonial Africa*. Durham, Duke University Press. 1996: 1.

Chapter Three

DRESS AND MATERIAL CULTURE

In the last decades of the nineteenth century the island of Sri Lanka was in some ways smaller than it is today. Men and women looked the same as they do now—as photographs taken by European travellers and colonial administrators seem to suggest—but they were probably physically slighter (figures in *Hue and Cry* give an average male height of persons taken in by the police as 5 feet in 1895). Their horizons too were limited—they were less literate and knew less about the rest of the world. However, this did not mean that their inner life was poorer.

We shall never know what their dreams were made of or what emotions they harboured—but that they dreamed their dreams, is certain. Life moved at a slower pace for the rural folk than for the city-dwellers. But if the large majority lived their lives in the village or the district of their birth, some moved and wandered away from their places of birth following the economic booms of the period—plumbago, graphite-mining and coconut. A few adventurous men and women even boarded ships that took them to Malaysia or Australia. They were part of the empire, subjects of the largest system of domination in the world. Of this world however they knew only a little through the fledgling Sinhala press, sporadic contacts with British government agents and through rumours that started in the workplace or in the tea boutique and spread at the speed of a bullock cart. The vagaries of a war in Europe or news of violence perpetrated on Muslims in the Orient, reached them but did not perturb them. But for those working in the new export industries, changes in the world economy were clearly felt. The First World War for instance, affected the growth of the coconut industry. The island was in that sense connected to the rest of the world through ties of domination and economic exchanges.

Colonialism had touched Ceylon in an uneven fashion. Only in the western and south-western regions of Ceylon had there been early signs announcing the burgeoning of modernity: the growth of towns, a moving labour force, the spread of the use of money, the rise in production and the expansion of long distance trade had broken the isolation and insularity of many people. Lives had become interconnected across territories, seas and oceans.

Changes which had commenced under the Portuguese and Dutch gathered momentum under British rule. The market society that developed, was dominated by the needs and demands of plantation capitalism (coffee, then tea, coconut, rubber) and commercial capitalism. The new export economy became an integral, though subordinate, part of a vast imperial network of production and exchange which was more or less coordinated and controlled by the metropolis in London. Within the island, the extension of capitalism was partial. Even if the use of money spread relatively rapidly and widely, norms and values of an earlier age did not cease to exist. Modernity touched everything, but like a light sprinkle of rain which people hardly felt. Tinned food was found and revelled in in the deepest rural hideaways. Ginger ale was consumed far away from centres of urban sophistication. There was of course a considerable regional variation in the degree to which the new institutions, norms and practices had spread. Modernity was not evenly distributed as it appears in the multifarious ways in which different social groups creatively recast the 'tradition/modernity' dichotomy imposed by colonialism, both transforming tradition and creating specific, local modernities.

45

This chapter will look at the changes in material culture during the end of the nineteenth and beginning of the twentieth century while focussing on the changes in dress—the wearing of dress and the making of dress—in order to understand the workings of the consumer culture in its early phase of development. In India, as in Ceylon, it was through the shift in urban taste that English fabrics and clothing styles gained a foothold in more rural markets. Modernity was not a purely urban phenomenon. Some of its artifices such as the sewing machine were accepted and sometimes welcomed and enthusiastically adopted by social groups which outwardly seemed steeped in tradition. These changes also generated resistances.

The Making of Dress: Sri Lanka's Dying Industry and British Textiles

Before the eighteenth century, many ships left from Venice to bring back cotton from Syria. It was later that cotton goods from India arrived in European markets. These were the 'calicos', the fine printed fabrics produced by skilful Indian weavers. Except for the Malabar coast which was rich in pepper, the textile industry was to be found in every region of India. Different sectors and circuits governed the production and marketing of raw materials: the manufacture of cotton yarn, weaving, bleaching and preparation of fabrics, and printing. All of India processed silk and cotton, sending a vast quantity of fabrics from the most extraordinary to the most luxurious all over the world. Until the English Industrial Revolution, the Indian cotton industry was the foremost in the world both in quantity of its output and the scale of its exports.[1] In the late seventeenth century India was one of the greatest producers and certainly the greatest exporter of cloth in the world. It was natural that Sri Lanka privileged trade with the subcontinent. Areca nuts, arrack, tobacco and coconuts from the island were among the items exported in return for such commodities as cloth and rice.[2]

Similarly, there had been scope in the eighteenth century, within the monopolistic regime maintained by the Dutch in the Maritime Provinces for coastal and inter-Asian trade, particularly with India.

The British conquered Sri Lanka in the nineteenth century. At this stage changes became evident in the textile trade. The cotton revolution in England, which began by imitating Indian industry, finally outstripped it. The aim of the British was to produce fabrics of comparable quality at cheaper prices. The only way was to introduce machines which alone could compete with Indian textile workers. Arkwright's water frame (1769) and Crompton's mule (1775–78) made it possible to produce yarn as fine and strong as the Indian product, one that could be used for weaving fabric entirely out of cotton. From then on the market for Indian cottons would be challenged by the developing English industry. The market covered was very large indeed: it stretched from England and the British Isles and Europe to the coast of Africa (where black slaves were exchanged for lengths of cotton), Turkey, the huge market of colonial America, and India itself.[3]

Sri Lanka soon became a destination for British cottons, albeit this was a small market. According to Ferguson, writing in 1887, Ceylonese farmers had always grown a little cotton in certain districts and at particular times, a sizeable amount of cotton cloth was manufactured at Batticaloa on the eastern coast but 'the industry has almost entirely ceased being driven out by the cheapness of Manchester goods … The result is that native cotton spinners and weavers are rare and the industry is dying out'. Even the little cotton that was produced—the short-stapled cotton from the pods of the silk-cotton tree—was, according to Ferguson, exported to

Australia and Europe to stuff chairs and mattresses.[4] But Ferguson, like many of his contemporaries, was not overly sentimental over the inevitability of the demise of traditional products which were seen to be incapable of competing in a modern world.

In 1906 Ethel Coomaraswamy wrote with more nostalgia of the by-gone age when cotton was still grown widely in Ceylon.

> The white or rather ivory coloured cotton which was used for the weaving of the cloth and also for embroidery was made by the people themselves. They grew the cotton (*Gossypium hernaceum*) cleaned and prepared it for spinning and spun it; probably they also made and dyed the coloured cottons, but the little that is used now in weaving is imported from India through Batticaloa.[5]

In the 1920s it was reported that experiments had been made with cotton in various parts of the colony by the government. There was some success in establishing an industry in the Hambantota district. Over 3,000 cwt of seed cotton[6] were produced during the 1925–26 season and found ready sale at the spinning and weaving mills in Colombo.[7]

This rather positive account by L.J.B. Turner must be weighed against the report of Dr C.A. Hewavitarne, Honorary Joint Secretary, Ceylon Cottage Industries Society who complained bitterly that under the British no Department of Handicrafts was set up although certain efforts were made to revive the 'dying industry'. His own society, established in 1922 with the aim of coordinating industries and encouraging craftsmen, received public as well as government support. He claimed there was an urgent need for this, for, except in Jaffna and Batticaloa, parts of Central Province and a few scattered spots in the maritime districts, weaving as an industry had died out.

The Technique

The looms (*alge*) were of very simple construction, the weaver sitting on the ground with his feet in a pit (*alvala*).

The shuttle was thrown by the hand to and fro while the alternate threads of the warp were separated by the needles which were hung up from a beam above. The *slay* or reed frame was also hung up from a beam above and consisted of a framework with thin slips of cane and bamboo for the warp thread to pass. The treadles were worked by the feet moving up and down inside the pit. Usually only two needles were used.[8]

48

Imports

By the early twentieth century with the exception of a small quantity of locally manufactured cotton cloth, most of the textiles needed in the island were important. The bulk consisted of cotton goods. During the two years preceding the First World War and the total import amounted to 14 million rupees. In 1920 it rose to 32 million and stabilised at 30 million in 1926.[9] There were of course exceptions: a merchant called A.B. Mathias de Silva from Matara was producing textiles on the put out system, importing yarn and supplying a bevy of weavers from whom presumably he received the finished products at fixed rates.[10]

The origin too of the goods imported underwent some changes. Half of the products still came from the United Kingdom and one-third from British colonies. But Japan and Germany sent a considerable proportion of the cheaper qualities of cotton clothes such as banians, shirts and under-garments. In bleached and printed piece goods England had a practical monopoly but imports of Japanese printed goods were on the rise. England and Holland supplied large quantities of sarongs, probably produced in Indonesia. In grey piece goods England supplied three-fourths of the quantity and the USA, British India and Japan, the remainder. Handkerchiefs, scarves and shawls came from the United Kingdom and Japan. Japan sent three-fifths of the total amount of silk and satin after British India. Even a few woollen goods were imported—blankets from British India, cloth stuff and flannel from the United Kingdom, scarves and shawls from Japan.[11] From the writings of the early twentieth century, the trade figures pointing to an influx of foreign goods, it was quite clear that Ceylon was now part of the world system and that the decline of its own already weak textile industry was irreversible.

Changing Lives

The lost battle waged by the local cotton production and local textiles against the forces of modernity was one aspect of the formidable social change that was sweeping across the island. Goods were transformed into commodities while consumption became an activity aimed at confirming who one was not—a rural/uncouth man or woman—rather than who one was.[12] The making of the meaning of commodities was a process that activated complicated struggles and negotiations between classes, genders and ethnicities and mediated relationships between the urban, peri-urban and rural worlds.

Moving people

In the 1901 census, for the first time information concerning the place of birth of the inhabitants of the island appeared: people were still very sedentary since 90 per cent lived in the district of their birth:

> The Ceylonese are not naturally of a roving disposition and they seldom leave their homes if without so doing they can procure a moderate subsistence.[13]

A few left for other lands. Most nineteenth-century Sinhalese migrants to Malaya, and Tanganyika, Uganda, Kenya, Siam, Shanghai, Hong Kong, Australia and Thursday Island were from Galle and Matara and their hinterlands in the southern coast of Ceylon. The Port of Galle in South Ceylon was the port for the schooners and steamships until the later part of the nineteenth century when with Ceylon's expanding tea industry; Colombo took precedence as a port. Foreign contact with sailors and captains probably provided information about the bountiful lands on these trade routes.

Most moved from one district to another. Economic activity in a district meant a larger portion of migrants hailing from other districts. In 1901 Puttalam had a rate of 33 per cent migrants essentially a workforce in connection with the extension of coconut plantation in the district. Half of these came from contiguous districts, Negombo and Chilaw. Between neighbouring districts boundaries were only geographical expressions. People moved from one village to another crossing boundaries oblivious to the fact that they would become a statistic in a census report. Between Matara and Hambantota, interdependence led to a flow to and fro. In 1905 the 'rubber mania' in Hambantota attracted many inhabitants from Matara.[14]

Twenty years later Kurunegala occupied the prime place in coconut plantation and 25.2 per cent of its population comprised migrants. From 1881 the trend was in place. During these years planters left Chilaw and Negombo to open up lands in two divisions of Kurunegala. For the clearing up of the lands men from the neighbouring districts flooded in. The next decade suffered a set-back due to the fever epidemic which decimated a large portion of the population. From 1901 the district grew again and prosperity followed. The surface of coconut plantations increased from 163,000 acres to 219,000 acres in the space of ten years. The division of Katugampola became the true centre of the coconut industry. Administrators signalled many and marked changes in the lifestyles of the population: for instance most of them lived in tiled buildings rather than in thatched ones as they had better means of earning and straw-thatched houses were rarely seen in the district.[15]

Although in 1911 the urban-rural divide was still pronounced with the large majority of the population living in rural areas, town life was no longer unknown to villagers. 'The wants of a town were created amongst the rural population.'[16] Wealthy villagers sent their children to school in the nearest large town. The isolation of the village had been breached with the new Colombo-Galle road and the coastal railway. But the fares of the railway in the late nineteenth century were such that older modes of transport survived. In 1895 carters were competing successfully over short distances with the southern railway in Galle. In the western province even in 1898, the bulk of Kalutara traffic to Colombo went by means other than railway. Most of the arrack and furniture produced in Kalutara and Moratuwa was transported in boats to Colombo.[17]

The city too was changing and growing. Of all the consequences of capitalism and colonialism in the late nineteenth and early twentieth century, the most visible in Sri Lanka was the growth of the city of Colombo. The expansion of the Colombo harbour and the building of a breakwater, which was completed in 1884, confirmed Colombo as the major business centre of the island. A massive demographic change followed. People migrated from the countryside to the city looking for employment and greater economic opportunities. From 1901–11 the Colombo rate of increase was more than double the island's rate.[18] In 1921 while the total population was 4,505,000, there were 15,000 villages and 33 principal towns out of which 11 had a population larger than 10,000. With urbanisation, modernity found a privileged terrain.

Turner described the changes that took place in the cities framing these changes quite predictably in the language of progress and development.

> Of the towns of Ceylon, the most important and progressive is the capital Colombo. It is the main business centre of the island, the seat of the government and its principal officials and the headquarters of the chief mercantile firms. It is consequently the most westernised of all the towns and possesses most of the refinements of modern civilisation, up-to-date hotels, electric lights, fans and tramways, an excellent water supply, an up-to-date system of water-borne drainage, an extensive emporia of goods of all kinds.[19]

Changes visible to the eye were witnessed in the houses built and renovated during this period. Until the early twentieth century tiled houses were not common in villages. The most common village house had a raised platform of earth with timber posts planted on the platform and a thatched roof on a framework of timber. The walls were usually of wattle and daub. In its simpler versions, both thatched screen walls and structures without walls could be seen. The most basic ground plan was rectangular with one or two rooms and an open verandah. Until 1818 when a British proclamation extended the privilege of having a tiled house to a larger group than the *adigars,* this privilege was confined to persons having a Commission for office signed by the Governor.[20] But in the first decades of the twentieth century the old mud-walled houses were gradually being replaced by tiled houses. Official sanction was given to this new development: 'It is a by-law of most local boards that every new house built must be tiled' testified Denham.[21] In Jaffna too, two- or three-roomed stone-built houses were a sign of prosperity.

For the richer families tiles were imported from British India: Mangalore tiles were in vogue. Granite slabs for the floor and country tiles in temples were traded for glazed flooring of European manufacture. Many of the pigments employed by temple artists—traditionally natural products such as roots and brick had been used—were imported from Europe.

Urban space became a competitive arena for presentational conflicts based on commercialised fashions and lifestyles.

Furniture

One of the few detailed accounts of the furniture in an 'ordinary villager's house' is given in Denham's Report of 1911. With the sense of detail of an apothecary he described the furniture in the house of a villager in the Colombo Mudaliyar's division.[22] The furniture was mainly functional but of good quality, for instance, a satin wood almairah and jakwood bed were mentioned. The walls had a few Buddhist pictures and the only concessions to frivolity were the mirrors, wine-glasses and clock. In Kalutara a villager's house contained pictures of the Buddha published and sent out by the Mellin's Food Company as an advertisement of their foods, together with a portrait of the late John Kotelawela. Mass-produced religious memorabilia was fast becoming, for commercial companies, a useful product for promoting their goods for mass consumption. The pictures on the walls in other simple households were also generally of a religious nature: saints or Virgin and Child or birth and renunciation of Prince Siddhartha. Pictures of Kings and Queens of Europe too were popular and available even in boutiques in interior villages. These images linked colonised subjects across the sub-continent in an imagined community of servants of the Raj.

In the house of a Vidana Arachchi, Japanese pictures hung on the walls. Western style hygiene was also entering the home with toilet tables in bedrooms, combs and powder boxes. The custom had been for long to have the toilet and bath-room separated from the rest of the house—this too was changing.

Highly perfumed soap was then in great demand. Even in the interior villages 'Cherry Blossom' and 'Famra' soap and powder were available in small boutiques and commanded a large sale. Soap was sold at 35c a cake and toilet powders at 40c a tin. Among the popular perfumed powders was one called 'White Rose,'[23] a name which married in one image the white colonial master and the rose, which evoked the gentle-ness of his civilisation. The irony was that the Sinhala villager had probably never smelt the fragrance of a rose. But through contact with cosmetics, the labouring body of the Sinhala man and woman became a desiring body. A letter to the editor of the *Sinhala Jatiya* castigated this new trend in women which was

> to waste money unnecessarily to beautify themselves, follow-ing the latest fashions and using strange things like perfume.[24]

This critique of wastage made a value judgment based on the distinction between necessities and luxuries. What was feared indeed was the gradual imposition of a consumer-culture as had happened in Europe. Modern consumption would produce a passive, subordinated population which would longer be able to realise its 'real needs.[25] Despite its critical tone, the analysis of consumerism often assumed a conservative stance. The argument that consumerism encourages narcissism can implicitly embrace a nostalgic adherence to the family, the work ethic and patriarchal authority.

Denham's interest in collecting such data reflects the colonial ruler's concern with the body of colonial subjects. Hygiene, domesticity and manner were only components in a larger network concerned with their bodies. The native body was an imagined subject that generated pervasive concern in official, settler and missionary discourse. Later in the twentieth century in Africa, institutional forms of communication, more advanced than in Sri Lanka in the early years of the century, were used to spread the gospel of cleanliness and other colonial forms of propaganda—demonstration and cinema vans, radio, African newspapers, women's clubs, health lectures, mission schools, beauty contests and fashion shows.[26] The spread of soaps and powders in rural Sri Lanka as well as more direct 'Lessons of Hygiene' in Africa were part of a general attempt to promote 'civilised' manners and discipline in the comportment of the self and the practice of everyday life in different colonial situations.

Food habits too changed with the import of foreign products. The middle classes drank imported gin, brandy and whisky and as one would expect, led the lifestyle of English gentlemen and women or what they thought was their lifestyle. Aerated waters were consumed commonly and manufacturers had sprung up in the island to meet the demand. Cream soda was among the most popular drinks. The consumption of meat increased considerably as the increase in the number of butchers and in the number of cattle thefts proved. At weddings of well-to-do villagers, meat was now being served. Festivals being celebrations of belonging and membership through the sharing of goods, the sharing of meat created a new basis for social interaction. Data is not available whether it was predominantly in Christian communities that meat was eaten. In the daily food of the people too changes were taking place: tea, coffee, and milk were gradually replacing *rice conjee* (cold rice water), and buttermilk. Tea boutiques were springing up everywhere especially near railways. The 100 per cent increase in the amount of preserved milk imported between 1901 and 1911 reflected the change in consumption habits. In the same way, people were using prepared foods for children such as malted milk and Mellin's and Allenbury's foods as this saved time. The

Ceylon described by Denham, was one at the threshold of the age of modernity where women went to work and spent minimal time in the kitchen. The popularity of tinned soups, meats and sardines was such that every bazaar was stocked with these products.

Perhaps as significant as the adoption of western types of food by the middle classes was the wholesale adoption of various south Indian foods such as *Appam* and *Iddi Appam* brought to Colombo by the Malayali migrant workers as virtual national foods. In matters of food the island was a crucible of influences.

From Weaving to the Sewing Machine

Even more than changes in food, the rural areas resolutely laid claims to modernity with the conquest of the sewing machine and the gramophone. While the gramophone, that had become visible in the colony through advertisement and showrooms, became a significant organising principle of a modern colonial private home in urban areas, the sewing machine could be found in the most remote rural areas of the island. It epitomised modernity: it was easy to work, faster than humankind and an instrument of standardisation. It could create replicable serials. In this sense it was as much part of the driving power of modernity as photography or print. With the sewing machine the human touch disappeared, the particular was replaced by the reproducible model.[27] Saree blouses for instance, could be made in vast quantities as each person had a block pattern to which the tailor referred. The sewing machine contributed to the *coup de grace* of traditional weaving by its art of replicating rather than creating unique products.

The Trade-companies

In the late nineteenth century a number of companies were vying for the market. Among them were Wrenn Bennet and Co which advertised 'the ideal sewing machine selling by thousands in England'.[28] But Singer was by far the most successful.

The first shop and office of the Singer Sewing Machine Company was established in Colombo in 1877 at No. 27 Main Street, Pettah. In 1851, Singer introduced the first practical sewing machine with two roller feeds. Subsequently it developed domestic straight stitch hand-operated models. The machines were marketed through Singer-owned retail outlets. After the first shop was set up in Pettah, branches were opened in Kandy, Galle and Hatton. Thereafter, the firmly-established Singer Sewing Machine Company opened branches in many towns throughout the island. People accepted the machines with open arms because Singer offered the sewing machine on easy payments from the inception. An advertisement in the Sinhala paper *Lakmina* warned against imitations and expounded the after-purchase servicing as well as the easy payment scheme.[29] The first users of these sewing machines were housewives and tailors. The first clothes sewn were jackets, shirts and sarongs.

A typical Singer advertisement went as follows:

> If you wish to reduce your tailoring expenses
> If you wish to save your time
> If you wish to see your family neatly dressed
> If you wish to see your ladies engaged in useful and intelligent
> work at home.[30]

The appeal was clearly to the housewife and displayed a conventional perception of what a useful occupation was for womenfolk. Indeed, at that time, middle-class women were getting involved in leisure activities—such as piano playing—which were not considered useful by many.

Some tailoring establishments such as Whiteaway Laidlaw & Co, Drapers and Outfitters, advertised themselves as users of sewing machines—an added proof of quality tailoring in 1918. With the conquest of the sewing machine the tailor too became modernised. Hannalis, the caste of Sinhalese tailors had never been numerous, since they worked mainly in the courts of the kings. In the early nineteenth century they were described by Davy as being 'very few'. A century later tailoring had mainly become the preserve of Tamils and Burghers as the newspaper advertisements indicate.[31]

Competing with Singer were other brands such as National and Pfaff. National advertised its product in the Sinhala newspapers:

> New National sewing machine
> No home is complete without this machine!

The machine was sold less as a useful item and more as a status symbol.[32] Pfaff sold it as an ideal Christmas present or wedding present.[33] The sewing machine would gradually become one of the main items in the dowry of a middle-class woman in Ceylon.

The appeal of the sewing machine also came from its unassuming size. Unlike other machines of the modern age such as trains or cars, the sewing machine was human in its size and appearance. Not long after Mahatma Gandhi issued a sweeping ban against the use of western machinery in India in the early 1920s he decided to make one exception: the sewing machine. The sewing machine, he explained after learning how to operate a Singer during a jail term, is one of the few useful machines invented.

Clothes and Fabrics

While the middle classes adopted the clothes and styles of the West, ordinary men and women bought the imported fabrics and made them to suit their own needs. The act of sewing was in itself a break with the past. Cloth, at least for women, had generally been worn wrapped around the body. Just as in India, sewn clothes were not vested with the same purity as wrapped cloth. For instance, Buddhist monks who were purported to be closer to *Nirvana* than the lay people, for instance, wore a cloth wrapped around their body.

In Sri Lanka though the predilection for unsewn clothes had been eroded even before this. The Portuguese and Dutch had introduced the sewn jacket for women worn with a wrapped cloth: in this dress both symbolic forms, the sewn and the wrapped were combined. Sinhalese men too attempted to merge tradition with modernity but in less attractive fashion by wearing a pair of western style trousers under their sarongs.

In India there was, by the nineteenth century, an appreciable shift towards European styles of clothing in the middle classes. Dress was an obvious marker of cultural change. The emergence of English style professions after 1850, with their emphasis on occupational rituals and conformity, also tended to break down resistance to European clothing and hence to English fabrics. Class formation and access to the resources of the colonial power both demanded an accommodation with Europe at least in the public arena. The most westernised were the professional men and government servants, while mercantile people were generally less.

This tendency spread to a much wider range of consumers in the 1870s when English textiles were made up into Indian styles by alert British merchants. Indians and Ceylonese bought British textiles, it has been asserted, because they were cheaper by 30–50 per cent than the indigenous ones and of finer quality. Apart from this utilitarian argument the spread of British products in the subcontinent was a reflection of a changing culture and political economy and not merely a response to better prices. Those Europeans who sold cloth to Indians were aware that taste and cultural preferences had to be accommodated.

In the early twentieth century the dress of men was becoming more and more assimilated to the fashions of the West. Consumerism even in its early incarnation democratised fashion but fashion was not always synonymous with western dress.[34] Indeed traditional dress—I use this term to describe dress forms which are in some way connected to the pre-colonial past of the country—often meant western clothing system halfway. The best example in the combination of sarong and trousers worn by some local leaders described in 1935 by Vijayatunga:

> ... the president of the village Tribunal ... wears a white cotton
> suit of the so-called European cut and wraps over his trousers
> a white cloth sarong-fashion in the native style, but leaving a
> good twelve inches of the trousers ends to be seen.[35]

58

Although Denham claimed that in 1911 this type of hybrid attire was no longer common it remained for many a way of being modern without offending tradition. Amongst the Tamils, the cotton cloth and shawl were gradually replaced by the coat and shirt and banian, especially among the younger men. Ordinary native-spun and Indian calico cloth were replaced by imported soft bleached cloth of a finer texture. Consumerism and fashion grew together. Earlier, the majority of the inhabitants of Sri Lanka were oblivious to fashion. The poor man's daily costume remained the same: for century upon century, from Jaffna to Matara, peasants wore a homespun cloth around their body and did not make any concessions to caprice. What Cordiner wrote in 1807 is still valid: 'they wear no clothing except a piece of cotton cloth folded round the waist.[36] The same can be said, however, about the Peruvian and the Indian who wore and still continue to wear *ponchos* and *dhotis*. In Sri Lanka little is known about the variations in men's dress during the precolonial period. Braudel speaks of a rule of changelessness which characterises oriental societies and suggests a correlation between the tendency of certain societies to care about changing colours, materials and shapes of costume and their success in changing the social order and the map of the world. His analysis that rests upon an orientalist reading of African and Asian societies can be both refuted and extended easily. What is argued about oriental societies is in fact applicable to rural people across continents. The dress of a French peasant from Auvergne would not have been in any way subject to fashion. Further, fashion as signifier of individuality, fantasy, play or seduction is not always the prerogative of the colonising power. A recent study of the dress of the Kikuyu in Kenya has shown that when modern dress arrived among the Kikuyu it became defashionised. Under settler colonials, African men wore a pair of tattered European trousers, a badly frayed shirt, a ragged woollen sweater, a threadbare suit coat and a floppy felt hat. Western clothing contrasted markedly to the lavish ornamentation and decorativeness of Kikuyu traditional dress.[38]

In Ceylon a concept of fashion was conceivable among the upper classes and the members of the court from ancient times as the island was constantly in contact with the Indian subcontinent where a variety of styles were regularly experimented with. Men and women of leisure had the time and resources to renew their wardrobes according to the products brought to them by tradesmen and gifts from friendly neighbours. Furthermore, colonialism brought new elements to the dress of the coastal inhabitants, especially the women, who adopted Dutch fashions such as lace collars and frills. But the late nineteenth century during which fashion and consumerism led on each other, provided a crucial break in the social mores of the people. The value of imports of hats and bonnets for instance increased by 141 per cent during the decade 1901–11 while the sales of lace and trimmings witnessed an important increase.[39]

Unlike the situation among the Kikuyu where western dress was defashionised and became the dress of the lumpen, in Ceylon, in the early twentieth century, western dress was the epitome of fashion. Those who wore western dress belonged mainly to the urbanised, educated, English-speaking male elites. Their status in society came with their lifestyle, that is an entirety of cultural practices where dress played an important part. As Bourdieu reminds us, status also involves and to a certain extent 'is style'.[40]

The extension of the franchise and the growth of mass consumer markets facilitated the decay of ascriptive signs of personal value. In early twentieth century Sri Lanka, self and the presentation of self became dependent on style and fashion rather than on fixed symbols of class and hierarchical status.

Resistances

The resistance to the colonisation of taste and the import of foreign goods took a number of divergent and often contradictory courses. The most significant protest emerged through the revivalist movement of the early twentieth century spearheaded by the lay preacher Anagarika Dharmapala. There were two components to this protest over dress and cloth. On the one hand, the movement encouraged Sinhalese men and women, as was mentioned in the previous chapter, to shed their western clothes and instead wear a native/ national dress. On the other, it was a movement meant at regenerating and modernising local industries so that they could compete with the West. Tradition and modernity were closely associated in this resistance as in most nativistic upsurges in Asia and Africa. Although its impact was limited in the early twentieth century compared to the mass movement that grew around the notion of *swadeshi* in India, the resistance to foreign goods had ramifications in the 1950s cultural break spearheaded by S.W.R.D. Bandaranaike.

Buying and Selling Patriotic Clothes

Advertising, a term coined in the late nineteenth century, 'enlarged and recontextualised the world of the object'.[41] Modes of representation in advertising share a certain strategy which consists in taking what are often perfectly ordinary, mass-produced, cheap products and making them seem somehow, in Simmel's sense, desirable yet reachable. The growth of the Sinhala press played an important part in the disseminating of advertisements. While nationalists of the day such as Venerable Shri Sumangala, Anagarika Dharmapala and Piyadasa Sirisena used their pen to attack western culture in newspapers such as *Lankalokaya, Lak Rivi Kirana, Lak Mini Pahana*, merchants and tradesmen advertised both national and imported goods in the same pages. In 1895 the first Sinhala daily, *Dinapata Pravrutti*, appeared.[42] This signalled a significant change in the insulated lives of most Ceylonese and led to the emergence of what Anderson has called a community in anonymity, a chain of readers who, every morning, performed the ritual of reading the same paper and the same advertisements.

As early as 1918 the saree was a marketable product as the advertisements for saree material in the press of the period clearly suggest. In this new arena, objects were managed and valued in modes radically different from those of the past. Many merchants did not hesitate to associate the saree quite overtly with patriotism. This advertisement by the Galle

Drapery Stores which appeared in 1913 in a Sinhala paper was quite typical:

> Clothing suited for our times
> For our ladies who dress in the Arya Sinhala style
> We remind you that we have brought down with great patriotism
> Silk osaris and various other fabrics very suitable for saris
> Very specially for you.[43]

Other products too were marketed as patriotic products:

> We are proud to announce that this is the famous Chandra Soap produced through much diligent hard work in Sri Lanka by us Sinhalese. We hope that all our patriotic ladies and gentlemen will give us their support in this venture.[44]

It is difficult to assess how new modes of communication —oral, visual, written and printed—inserted themselves into contemporary consciousness. Most probably through the press, early nationalists, who belonged to the literate merchant classes, knew something about the Swadeshi movement that was taking Bengal by storm in the wake of its Partition. To quantitatively measure the influence of India is more difficult. Boycott of British products was never an instrument of national resistance but then there was little resistance to speak of. Unlike in India where bonfires of foreign clothes were organised at Poona on 8 October 1905, swadeshi in Sri Lanka did not go beyond a solitary act of an individual in search of self-esteem. The main object of the nationalists was indeed to make Sinhalese people proud of their own products, culture and habits. They did not seek to rally crowds or fight for independence. The same shops that were selling patriotic goods also sold items which were virulently condemned by more traditional Sinhalese nationalists. Among such objects featured in newspapers were brassieres ... which some Sinhalese men felt were dangerous items of clothing possibly leading to 'suffocation of their women' and impeding the production of milk for breastfeeding.[45]

A large drapery store in Galle would advertise osari cloth as well as silk cloth 'suitable for shirts,' as well as dresses, veils, brassieres, hats, socks and shoes.[46]

The idea of boycotting foreign goods were present in Anagarika Dharmapala's condemnation of imported goods but it never acquired a central place in his programme:

> We purchase Pears soap, and eat coconut biscuits manufactured by Huntley and Palmer, and sit in chairs made in Austria, drink the putrefied liquid known as tinned milk manufactured somewhere in the South Pole, while our cows are dying for want of fodder ... and our own brass lamps we have melted and are paying to purchase Hinks lamps which require ... chimneys manufactured in Belgium. Our own weavers are starving and we are purchasing cloth manufactured elsewhere.[47]

63

When he wrote these lines Dharmapala was clearly influenced by the boycott, *swadeshi* and *swaraj* concepts which were forged in Bengal during the anti-partition protests. During that period, orders for English goods, particularly textiles, were cancelled in Calcutta. The campaign to boycott English goods was matched by the call to use locally manufactured products. This was particularly striking in the case of textiles. Handweaving of cloth was a cottage industry in Bengal which was languishing due to the influx of manufactured cloth from Britain. The anti-British agitators gave up western cloth (associated with sin) and adopted a homespun or *khadi* national costume which became a rallying point of the entire freedom movement. Gandhi who was behind this recreation of Indian dress offered in khadi his own resolution to the problem of the divided self that threatened Indian identity under British rule.[48]

Having spent forty-one years of his life in India, it was not surprising that the idiom and nature of Dharmapala's protest grew out of his Indian encounters and experiences. But this explains perhaps why the movement did not take off in Sri Lanka. Dharmapala was using a language and symbols which were alien to most Ceylonese. For them, modernity was not, as in India, a phenomenon seen in culturally traditional and purist terms. It was rather the product of fortuitous encounters with other civilisations which were received and absorbed in an unabashedly unreflective manner.

Regenerating Traditional Industries

In 1906, Ethel Coomaraswamy wrote a long and detailed article on 'Old Sinhalese Embroidery'. On a visit to Haldummulla, she had come across a beautifully embroidered betel bag of blue cotton which belonged to a former Arachchi, and had marvelled at the workmanship. This was an eye-opener for her. She wrote with a touching naiveté:

> Many other things I also found out. How that it is to modern conditions of life that this fine art has fallen into decay ... ; the cloth cannot be got, the cottons cannot be bought, and the things that used to be made have gone out of fashion.

The nostalgia was for indigenously produced goods from the beginning of the production process until the end.

> The cotton was grown by the people themselves, they used to dye it with home-made dyes and weave it into the cloth they wanted. Now all this is past; the fine blue handmade cotton cloth that used to be universal, is now to be obtained only with the greatest difficulty, if at all. It is no longer made and dyed by the Sinhalese themselves. They still make the undyed cloth in a few districts, but that is not at all easy to obtain.[49]

Ethel Coomaraswamy and many other middle-class men and women were aware that modernity was destroying some beautiful crafts and products of the past but they failed to transform their feelings into action. The leaders of the Temperance Movement were the only individuals who took concrete steps: the Hewavitarne Industrial Centre was founded by Anagarika Dharmapala and Walisinha Harischandra in 1912 as the first industrial training school in the country. It offered a variety of courses which only a few institutions could offer. In addition to the normal courses of study there was weaving, pottery, sewing and similar arts and crafts.

The school was not reminiscent in any way of a Gandhian ashram but was modelled on the industrial schools Dharmapala had visited in the United States, England, Italy and Denmark. In 1904 he had commenced an industrial training school in Saranath, personally financed the entire training of U.B. Dolahapillai and sent him for industrial training to Japan. Dolahapillai subsequently became the Principal of that institution.

Technological change was an important feature of the school. An improved fly shuttle loom was first introduced in 1913 when the Hewavitharana Weaving School opened in Colombo. With this method the output increased three or four times. It spread to Jaffna and Batticaloa. The hand loom used was a modification of the English hand loom.

While modern methods were being tested, home-spun thread using the *chakra* was also introduced at the school. The chakra consisted of a wheel turned by handle and a spindle which revolved by means of a driving band. The cotton 'wick' was pushed to the point of the spindle and then spun into the yarn which rolled around the spindle.[50]

In 1917, state sponsorship of a kind was given to the handloom textile industry. That year the education department trained two scholars abroad and in 1921 the Education Department started a government weaving school at Talpawila and a school at Batticaloa. In 1942 there were in addition to a training institute at the Technical College, 16 government weaving schools and 12 assisted weaving schools. It was in 1936 during the Donoughmore experience in self-government that the Department of Commerce and Industries first began to interest itself in handloom textiles. Demonstration centres were started based on the model of India. Its aims were:

> to demonstrate to learners modern methods of processing,
> to provide facilities for deserving workers in the locality,
> to provide officers to visit homes or institutions in the locality
> and to give the necessary advice and instruction,
> to encourage and assist workers to buy their own machinery
> such as looms on easy terms,
> generally to give whatever assistance is necessary to encour-
> age and promote the textile industry.[51]

These measures had the double effect of reviving the cottage industry and killing its political potential. Unlike India where articulate and sustained opposition to British imports took fire in the late nineteenth century, Ceylon had no history of boycott. Dharmapala's resistance to colonial goods was intended to produce goods of an industrial nature which were compatible with his idea of what should be part of the national heritage. He was in this sense the ultimate modernist.

After him, there were a few attempts by the Ceylon National Congress (CNC) to promote swadeshi goods through swadeshi exhibitions in a non-confrontational manner. In 1941 the CNC organised a Swaraj Exhibition in Wennapuwa during the 22nd session of the Congress. The president arrived clad in national dress and the majority of the delegates were in cloth and banian. All the exhibits were manufactured or produced in Ceylon. Among the textiles were clothes, towels, dusters, comboys, sarongs, shirtings, silk cloths, sarees, curtain cloths, handloom and mill cloths.[52] Swadeshi, however, never became a rallying call for mass mobilisation.

Just like the national dress that in the minutes of the CNC is quite typically referred to as 'national costume', swadeshi remained at the level of exhibit.

NOTES

1. F. Braudel. *Civilisation and Capitalism, Fifteenth–Eighteenth Century, Vol. I. The Structures of Everyday Life.* London: Collins. 1984: 327.

2. M. Roberts. 'Elite Formation and Elites, 1832–1931'. In M. Roberts (ed). *Collective Identities Re-visited,* Vol. I. : 196.

3. F. Braudel. *Op. cit.*: 571–74.

4. John Ferguson. *Ceylon in the Jubilee Year.* A.M.J. Ferguson, Colombo, 1887: 55.

5. E. Coomaraswamy. 'Textiles and Embroidery'. *Ceylon National Review.* I, 2, July, 1906: 10.

6. Cwt means a hundred weight. One hundred weight is equal to 112 pounds.

7. L.J.B. Turner. *Handbook of Commercial and General Information for Ceylon.* Colombo, M. Ross Cottle, Government Printer, Ceylon 1927: 132.

8. Coomaraswamy. *Op.cit.*: 121

9. Turner. *Op.cit.*: 42

10. Roberts. *Op.cit.*:200

11. Turner. *Op.cit.*: 43
12. C. Campbell. 'The Meaning of Objects and the Meaning of Actions'. *Journal of Material Culture*. I: 1, 1996: 93–105.
13. *The Census of Ceylon 1901. Vol. I, Review of the results of the Census of Ceylon.* 1901: 118.
14. *Administration Report of the Government Agent, Southern Province.* 1905: 4.
15. E.B. Denham, *Op.cit*: 95.
16. *Ibid*: 158.

67

17. *The Ceylon Observer.* 4 December 1897. CO 54/580, Under-Secretary of State 10 July 1888; Ceylon Administrative Report. 1895.
18. B.L. Panditaratne. 'Trends of Urbanisation in Ceylon: 1901–53'. *The Ceylon Journal* of *Historical and Social Studies.* 7: 2 July–December 1964: 206.
19. Turner. *op.cit.*: 4.
20. The Adigar was the chief officer of state in the Kandyan kingdom.
21. E.B. Denham: *Ceylon at the Census of 1911.* Government Printer, Ceylon: 159.
22. The Mudaliyar was the chief headman and the administrator of a Korale in British times.
23. E.B. Denham: *Ceylon at the Census of 1911.* Government Printer, Ceylon: 170.
24. *The Sinhala Jatiya.* 1 February 1923.
25. Much recent analysis of consumption is in this respect, largely negative. The critique of modern leisure and consumption tends to be nearly puritanical, neglecting the element of personal freedom which modern technology makes possible. The critique of consumerism is thus often a version of the dominant ideology thesis. It is simply not the case, however, that consumers inevitably absorb the meaning and purpose of mass advertisements.
26. T. Burke 'Sunlight Soap has Changed My Life: Hygiene, Commodification, and the Body in Colonial Zimbabwe'. In H. Hendrickson (ed.). *Clothing and Difference: Embodied Identities in Colonial and Post-Colonial Africa.* Durham Duke University Press. 1996: 189–212.
27. B. Anderson. *Imagined Communities. Reflections on the Origin and the Spread of Nationalism.* Revised and extended edition second ed: London and New York, Verso. 1991: 182–83.
28. *The Ceylon Examiner.* 23 March 1896: 1.
29. *Lakmina.* 4 January 1895: 1

30. *The Ceylon Independent.* 6 February 1904: 10.

31. Bryce Ryan. *Caste in Modern Ceylon.* (2nd edn). New Delhi: Navrang. 1993: 113–14.

32. *Lakmina.* 19 January 1918: 4.

33. *The Ceylon Independent.* 6 February 1903: 7.

34. Writers on western fashion from Baudelaire to Gilles Lipotevsky describe it as a paradigm of modernity. By extension, the concept of fashion is, in their analyses, absent in traditional societies. This interpretation needs further scrutiny.

35. Cited in Emma Tarlo. *Clothing Matters: Dress and Identity in India.* New Delhi: Viking. 1996; 49.

36. J. Cordiner. *Description of Ceylon Containing an Account of the Country. Inhabitants and Natural Productions.* Vol. 1. (First published 1807.) Rpt. Dehiwala, Tisara Prakasayo, 1993:55.

37. Braudel. *Op.cit.*:

38. Leslie W. Rabina. 'Not a Mere Ornament: Tradition, Modernity, and Colonialism in Kenyan and Western Clothing'. *Fashion Theory. The Journal of Dress, Body and Culture.* 1: 2, June 1997: 156.

39. Denham: *Op.cit.* 169.

40. P. Bourdieu. *Distinction: A Social Critique of the Judgment of Taste.* London: Routledge & Kegan Paul. 1984.

41. C.A. Breckenbridge. 'The Aesthetics and Politics of Colonial Collecting: India at the World Fairs'. *Comparative Studies of Society and History.* 31: 2, 1989: 201.

42. N. Karunanayake (ed.). *The Press in Sri Lanka. Towards a Sound Policy Framework.* Nugegoda, Media Publication. 1996.

43. *Arya Sinhala Wansaya.* 21 January 1913.

44. *Arya Sinhala Wansaya.* 18 February 1918.

45. *Sinhala Jatiya.* 27 May 1913.

46. *Arya Sinhala Wansaya.* 25 November 1913.

47. A Guruge (ed.). *Anagarika Dharmapala: Return to Righteousness.* Colombo, 1965: 509.

48. Tarlo: *Op.cit*: 62–93.

49. Coomaraswamy. *Op.cit.*: 119–20.

50. *British Empire Exhibition 1924. The Official Handbook.* Colombo, Colombo Apothecaries, 1924: 154–55.

51. *The Ceylon Trade Journal.* VII: 4 April 1942.

52. M Roberts (ed.). *Documents of the Ceylon National Congress and Nationalist Politics in Ceylon, 1929–50.* II. Colombo, Department of National Archives, 1977: 1418–40.

Chapter Four

IMAGINED AUTHENTICITIES: DRESS, COLONIAL MINDS, COLONISED BODIES

New nation-states grow as much from shared histories, fantasies and myths retold as from flags, songs and national costumes reinvented. Braudel speaks of 'certain stock images' and 'certain passwords known to the initiated' in which a nation recognises itself and 'of a thousand touchstones, beliefs, ways of speech, excuses, and an unbounded subconscious...'.[1] In this sense, before the cesure that comes with independence, a number of voluntary and contingent forces work in concert to weave an authentic self for the various communities which constitute the nation-state. Authenticity can be likened to a collective dream which calls for material proof. Dress, which is visible, tangible and reproducible, plays an important role in the consolidation of nations. In Ceylon paradoxically, it was late British colonialism that helped shape and define the features of what was to constitute the authentic in the nation-state, through the drawing up of boundaries between communities and the officialising of certain symbolic communitarian traits. Dress provides a fascinating lens for discovering the often contradictory components of authenticity.

Whose Authenticity? Colonial Writings and Boundaries

In Ceylon, elites of various communities began to articulate their concern for tradition and authenticity when colonialism showed signs of faltering. Before that, customs, practices, food and dress habits of visitors and conquerors were absorbed and transformed with little reflective feelings of guilt. The search for authenticity which occupied the early twentieth century was one which each community in the island lived in different ways, but in each case, the definition of the self involved redefining or sharpening boundaries between the self and the other. To this fashioning of authenticities, colonialism contributed in a significant manner.

Mostly what the British brought about was a new way of looking at identities. Identities were no longer substance that took many forms and shapes, they became objective features of people that could be once and for all delineated. This in itself did not change the shape of the varied and contextual identities of the peoples of the land but it led to the gradual imposition of the idea that identities were like institutions, fixed and gelled. One of the conventions in census is the 'impermissibility of fractions, or to put it the other way round, the mirage-like integrity of the body'.[2] It also moored the belief that by claiming belonging to one or another group recognised by the colonial rulers, one could obtain certain entitlements. In that sense colonial knowledge did not imagine identities or construct them, rather it opened up a new realm for political identities to blossom.

During the late colonial period, colonial subjects were beginning to create for themselves a public arena with the growth of the press and the emergence of the modern theatre and novel. Simultaneously, the colonisers' concern for collecting, collating and publishing, for official as well as scholarly use, detailed information about all aspects of the population acquired a new dimension. There had been, at first, a feeling of confusion and marvel at the diversity of the peoples living in the island on the part of the early British visitors and colonisers. Percival's description of the different 'castes', 'races', 'mixed races', 'half castes', 'religions', 'languages', 'classes of people' each with their own 'manners, customs and language' in the city of Colombo in 1803 revealed the difficulties he and his contemporaries faced when they attempted to make sense of human differences.[3]

71

Censuses, gazetteers, administrative reports were, at that time, carefully written from first hand observation. However in time, this concern became part of an imperial project of control where natives were counted, objectified and divided into social groups such as castes, races or ethnic groups. British colonialism did not in any sense of the term invent or imagine identities. What colonial officials were trying to do in their writings and policies, in an often clumsy way was to 'describe something that had practical and conceptual coherence both for outsiders and observers and the peoples of Sri Lanka themselves. Neither were the British the first to use such enumerative technologies in this manner: both the Portuguese and the Dutch had made great efforts in compiling *tombos*, or lists of persons and lands. Furthermore they too produced labels for the communities and social groups they encountered. Indeed the Portuguese and Dutch officials and writers used certain categories to describe the peoples they encountered which were very similar to those later used by the British in the nineteenth century. Mission reports of Dutch priests in the eighteenth century refer to 'Tamil' and 'Chingala' people and the sect of Budu 'which is the religion of all the Chingalas of Ceilao'.[4]

But where the British differed was in the systematic manner that this listing was done and the stamp that was given to identities as providing the basis of entitlements and rights such as places in the administration or representation in the Legislative Council. The process of objectification was based on the way natives represented themselves to the British, and what little knowledge the British were able to gather from native informants. Thus Anderson's claim that the nineteenth century colonial state dialectically engendered the grammar of the nationalisms that eventually arose to combat it, needs to be nuanced in the light of recent criticisms of the constructivist position on identity.[5]

The extent to which the construction of knowledge about the peoples of Sri Lanka by its European colonisers would have influenced the ways in which individuals and communities perceived themselves is difficult to assess. Identities were constantly in flux and took different shapes according to the practices—religious, educational, political—that they enacted. It is quite likely that the majority of the population would have remained for long unconcerned by colonial categories of classification that were made in the law and in the administration until they themselves were involved in a process where they had to define themselves according to these categories.

In Ceylon among the apparatus of knowledge destined to guide the British ruler in his dealings with the natives the census stood out as a document whose manifest rhetoric was technical but whose subtext was contestory and disciplinary.

The purpose of the first censuses in Ceylon was solely to find out the number of natives in the colonised territory. As there were no regular registers of the population, enumerations were merely approximations. In 1789, by the order of Governor Vander Graff, the first census was made in Ceylon. It covered all the inhabitants in the Dutch East India Company (the Maritime Provinces), and the population enumerated was 817,000. As the census was taken for the purpose of taxation, serious inaccuracies in the count were expected. The next estimate by Bertolaccai, based on food consumption, gave the population of the Maritime Provinces as 700,000 between 1808 and 1810.

With the demise of the Kandyan kingdom in 1815, the entire island, was for the first time, subject to western political control. The integrity of Ceylon as an administrative unit was reinforced by its separation in 1802 from British India.

The new administrators soon set about to collect systematic information about various aspects of Ceylonese society and economy. Unlike in India where a Gazetteer was first produced in 1820 and city censuses were conducted before officials tried launching into an all-India census collection, in Ceylon the scale of the country permitted the carrying out of a census of a larger territory.[6] Thus, in 1814, following a severe famine in the British territory, a census was conducted which reported the population as only 492,000.[7]

73

In the newly-annexed Kandyan provinces, a census was taken in 1821 which gave the population as 257,000. In an 1824 census, published in 1827 under Governor Barnes the population of all the provinces under British rule was found to be 890,000. This census was taken at the time of the suppression by the British of a rebellion in the Kandyan province which decimated a number of villages. Its results were unlikely to be accurate.[8]

No complete census was taken until 1871. Indeed, it is only in 1868 that the first Census Ordinance was passed to provide for the taking of a census when the Governor with the advice of the Executive Council should deem necessary.[9] However, returns submitted by the government agents provided annual estimates at the district level which were published in the *Blue Books*. These returns were more often based on information provided by the village headman. In a few cases a sample census was made. It appears that the population resented giving information, as Governor Torrington's experience testifies. His zealous effort to collect first-hand information seems to have been, according to Tennent's evidence before the Select Committee, one of the causes of a revolt in 1848.[10]

The first modern census taken in 1871 produced some unusual reactions on the part of a population still unaccustomed to being counted. Sarkar reports thus:

Many people fled from their villages and spent weeks in the forests; others hastily got married and even took the unusual step of getting their marriage registered. The panic arose from a wide-spread rumour that the purpose for the counting was to transport younger males to Europe to make good the depletion in manpower caused by the Franco-Prussian war.[11]

In India, the same year, a census of most of the provinces and princely states was carried out. The official rationale for the taking of the census in India and in Ceylon was based on administrative necessity. In 1871, a census was also carried out simultaneously in Great Britain and Ireland. The Registrar-General was charged with the conduct of the census but the actual work of enumeration was done by the Government agents and their assistants. Enumerators were selected at the district level.[12] As Smith has pointed out in his study of British imperial rule of law in India, village records, district records and census reports were meant to provide a photograph of the actual state of the community.[13] In Ceylon, too, the purpose of the census was to give an authorised version of knowledge about society.

Colonial Categories and the Authentic

There was a tremendous amount of experimentation on categories. When the British officials chose to delineate groups within the native population and refer to them as castes, nationalities, races or communal groups, the term used was never innocent or fortuitous; it reflected an understanding of the differences prevalent among the people of Ceylon. Throughout British rule, in spite of the vagaries in the categories chosen, the underlying principle remained the same: natives were members of a distinct group, their behaviour, needs, features were those of this group. India's population, just as Ceylon's, was not a collection of individuals. As Cohn has pointed out in the case of India, the British needed labels which served to locate the strange in a frame of reference with which they were familiar. This entailed arranging groups in neat diagrams, or in alphabetical order, simplifying them, and finding equivalents in language: for instance, Brahmins became priests, just as Goyigamas became farmers. Groups were reified.

D.S. Senanayake in top hat, 1948.

Independence Day, 4 February 1948.

S.W.R.D. Bandaranaike in national dress in the State Council, 1936.

S.W.R.D. Bandaranaike at the *chakra* as a young man.

Family photograph, early twentieth century.

Kandyan family; lady in osariya.

Sinhalese women picking coffee.

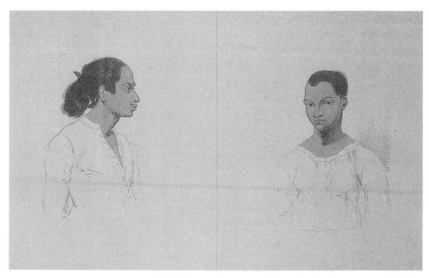

A Sinhalese man and woman.

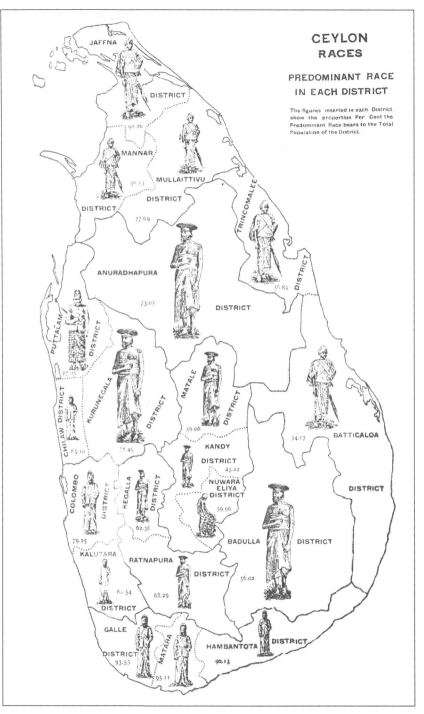

Ceylon: Races (Predominant race in each district).

A Malay.

A Muslim 'Tamby' commonly referred to
as a Moor.

Kandyan Mudaliyar.

A Sinhalese man with a *konde*.

Portrait of Maha Mudaliyar Don
Solomon Dias Bandaranaike.

D.A.L. Perera reproducing the Sigiriya frescoes.

D.A.L. Perera in Muhandiram costume.

H.C.P. Bell and his labour force.

The 1814 census as well as the 1824 census give information on castes and religions in Ceylon. Caste was the category used to differentiate groups in these censuses, just as in the censuses in India. But in Ceylon, the term 'caste' was more vague. It encompassed caste groups not only in their most recognised sense such as Vellalas,[14] but also regional groups such as Europeans, Portuguese and Malays; occupational groups such as washers or potters, and large amorphous groups such as Moors and Malabars, for example.[15]

It seemed that at least until 1824 Sinhalese and Tamils were perceived not as clear-cut ethnic groups but first and foremost as members of a number of caste groups of various sizes.[16] Caste particulars in censuses were not obtained because, according to Denham, 'caste does not play in Ceylon the important part it does in India.'[17]

In 1835, a detailed statement of the total population was prepared from headmen returns, registers of births and deaths. The population was grouped under the following heads: whites (9,121), free blacks (1,194,482), slaves (27,397) and aliens and resident strangers (10,825).[18] These categories were not castes but they expressed more clearly the feeling of exclusion-inclusion which permeated colonial situations. The British were whites. The 'others' were their anti-thesis, blacks, an all-encompassing term.

In 1871 and 1881 censuses the term 'race' appeared for the first time along with the category of nationality.

In 1871 there were seventy-eight nationalities and twenty-four races. There was a certain amount of incoherence in these classifications: Sinhalese and Tamil, for instance, were races as well as nationalities. It seems that the category nationality was introduced to describe groups numerically too small to be called races, for instance, Abyssinian or West Indian. The 1881 census showed a process of rationalisation: there were only seven races left, namely, Europeans, Sinhalese, Tamils, Moormen, Malays, Veddas and 'others'. The number of nationalities had slightly decreased from seventy-eight to seventy-one. From then on, race became the main category of classification.[19]

The term 'nationality' which entered the official usage in the middle of the nineteenth century at the time nationalities were awakening in western Europe, was dropped in 1911 in favour of the new term 'race'. Denham explains the reasons which led to the adoption of the category of race instead:

> In spite of the former use of the word 'nationality', it cannot be regarded as an appropriate description of the various peoples in Ceylon. The races in Ceylon are clearly differenti-ated—intermarriage between them have been very rare; they have each their own particular religion to which the large majority belong and they speak different languages. But of the races which are the most numerous in Ceylon—Sinhalese, Tamils, Moors, Malays, Burghers and British—only one race can regard Ceylon as the home of the nation and the shrine of its national traditions.[20]

Developments in physical anthropology and linguistics at the turn of the twentieth century were responsible for the definition of essentially linguistic groups such as Tamil and Sinhalese in Ceylon in terms of physical characteristics which were supposed to be specific to those groups. Thus, Denham, exemplifying the dangerous confusion between biological and cultural concepts, could write confidentially:

> It is remarkable that the race of the earliest settlers should have been preserved to the extent it has, for it is clear to the most superficial observer that there are very marked physical differences between the Sinhalese and the Tamils.'[21]

There was also a general consensus among the exponents of racial theories such as Kunte, Virchow, C.F. and P.B. Sarasin at the end of the nineteenth century that the Sinhalese were Aryans or a mixed race derived from the fusion of the Aryans and the aboriginal inhabitants of the island, and that the Tamils were distinct from them.[22]

British administrators were not solely responsible for the introduction of racial ideas in Ceylon. A.J. Wilson points out that German scholars such as Max Muller and Wilhelm Geiger played an important role in infusing the cultural movements of the early twentieth century with racial undertones.[23]

The number of races in the censuses also increased. The 1921 Census recognised ten principal races in Ceylon, three pairs being subdivisions of larger groups. These pairs were the Low-Country and Kandyan Sinhalese, the Ceylon and Indian Tamils, and the Ceylon and Indian Moors. The four other specified races were: the Burghers and Eurasians and the Malays and Veddas. The differentiation of the Sinhalese community into Low-Country and Kandyan Sinhalese, a division that was regional in origin, was a legacy of the European impact. The Low-Country Sinhalese of the southern and western coastal areas, more than two-thirds of the Sinhalese tended, as a result of four centuries of western influence, to diverge somewhat in social practices and attitudes from the more traditional Kandyans of the interior, who remained independent until 1815 and were subject to western influences to a lesser degree. This was the rationale for dividing the Sinhalese into two distinct groups. In the same way, the predominantly Saivite Hindu Tamils who lived in the Northern Provinces, in the Jaffna peninsula, along the east coast and in the city of Colombo, were called Ceylon Tamils so as to distinguish them from the Tamil-speaking South Indians who had come in the nineteenth century as temporary sojourners in search of employment on the tea and rubber plantations of the interior hill-country or to work as labourers in the towns. This group was referred to as Indian Tamils. Censuses also divided the island's Muslims into three separate communities. Under the category Ceylon Moors were Muslims living along the coast in the Eastern Province, in Colombo, and in the cities of the west coast. The category Indian Moors encompassed more recent Muslim migrants from India. The category Malays drew under its fold Muslims who claimed descent from East Indies troops brought to Ceylon by the Dutch. In terms of origins, both Muslims and Tamils of the Eastern Province had hailed from the southern coast of India. Religion had demarcated these two groups.

Although the larger categories of race became acceptable by the people, caste remained as an important feature of classification upon which colonial constructions had little effect. Some caste categories simply disappeared. This was the case of the Hammaru, the caste of tanners, present in the writings of early nineteenth century travellers but invisible thereafter.

Other castes, such as the Batgam, absorbed in their fold new groups growing into large communities. There were also contests over the caste hierarchy as it appeared in government documents and which most administrators accepted as a given. The main contest involved the Goyigamas and the Karava, Salagama and Durava castes of the coastal belt. The British administration's policy had in the first decades of the nineteenth century officially recognised the existence of higher castes and lower castes in the choice of juries—the distinction was between 'first class' and 'second class'—or in the selection of headmen. But after the abolition of *rajakariya* and petitions on the part of the 'second class' men, the recognition of caste was abolished in the selection of juries in 1844. The new opportunities which emergd with the growth of a capitalist export economy led non-Goyigama castes to compete for public employment. The end of the nineteenth century witnessed a growth in caste tensions which manifested itself in altercations, judicial disputes, and petitions to the government. The position of the colonial administration varied from encouragement to emerging castes such as Karavas, Salagamas and Duravas by giving them official posts at the district level (Korale Mudaliyar) to openly favouring Goyigamas conceived as the 'native aristocracy'.

Thus although the colonial census played a crucial role in drawing discrete boundaries between communities and gelling identities which were until then flexible and contextual, conflicts and resistances to these classifications constantly transformed a seemingly ordered picture. In the Sinhalese community, although the colonial understanding of caste categories was generally accepted, elites of these groups contested the dominance of the Goyigamas and the state patronage given to them.

Colonial Constructions of Authenticity

However radical the changes may be which are taking place in the manners and customs of the country, any attempt to understand the character, prejudices and outlook of an Eastern people must be based on a realisation of the innate conservatism of the East.[24]

In colonial Ceylon as in other parts of the Raj, 'the Oriental' was perceived as strange, primal and anti-modern. He was thus seen as conservative, hostile to new ideas, stuck in a world which had stopped evolving and had been left behind by the more dynamic western countries. By the nineteenth century, however, 'the Orient' was no longer inscrutable, rather it was there, predictable and ready to be discovered. The reawakening of the East would be done with the benevolent help of the British—while Europe was progressive, Ceylon was static. But, strangely, the static and unchanging was also valued more than the modern.

The Dress of Chiefs: Official Authenticities

Colonial rulers participated in defining what was authentically Sinhalese, Tamil, and Muslim 'in an official and objective sense' as B.S. Cohn explains, speaking of the similar situation in India where 'Indians had to look like Indians'. The imperial rulers in India gradually defined and expropriated Indian civilisation. After 1860, for instance, Indian and English soldiers ceased to wear western style uniforms and adopted turbans, sashes and tunics which conformed to the British vision of what was Mughal or Indian.[25] In Ceylon, however, Ceylonese were not made to look like Ceylonese. British rule did not participate in creating a uniform Ceylonese model. On the contrary, the specificity of each ethnic group, Low-Country Sinhalese, Kandyan Sinhalese, Tamil, and Muslim, was emphasised. Instructions regarding the number of appointments for each group, to the office of headman, president of the village tribunal or interpreter to the governor, and to honorary ranks as Mudaliyar, Muhandiram or Adigar were laid out in 1935. Honorary ranks were generally bestowed on occasions such as the King's birthday. Many of these ranks did not have antiquity to commend them. The Muhandiram rank for the Tamils was created in 1935. Legitimacy was brought to these offices and titles through the institution of a strict etiquette.

In fact the British inherited from the Dutch the custom of legislating over issues of dress and costume and gelling what they believed were the authentic features of castes or races. Kotelawela cites a petition of a group of 'washers' who were converts of the Dutch reformed Church but who used the caste myths of origin to appeal to the Dutch government for the permission to wear coats and hats for men and stockings for women.[26] There were also more general Dutch restrictive regulations such as the 1686 'Order to the Chingalese in general and to the low castes in particular to observe in their clothing the customs, laws and manners of the country'.[27]

80

In British Ceylon, for the attendance of every public function, details of the appropriate headwear, footwear, medals and swords were given: a Tamil Muhandiram had to wear a white turban with silver lace and a Muslim Muhandiram a Turkish turban with white as the predominant colour. Uniforms were exotic exhibits of the 'authentic' indigenous cultures, as the British perceived them. Nothing western was tolerated in the dress of Ceylonese officials; hence the following description of the shirt a president of a village committee had to wear: 'white frills (not to be European dress shirt).'[28] Amusingly, when the etiquette was breached such as in a 1938 Buckingham Palace reception when Peiris, a Sinhalese of the Low-Country, wore a uniform similar to one of a Kandyan chief, the British felt outraged. The O.A.G. referred to Peiris disparagingly as 'a member of the Karava community of inferior social status in no way related to the Kandyans.'[29] A dress etiquette for native headmen had been institutionalised along caste lines in the early days of British rule in Ceylon. The following caste categories were delineated: Vellala Fishermen and Chandoos, Blacksmith and Washermen, Barber. For each caste, details were given as to how headmen of differahaent ranks—Maha Mudaliyars, Muhandirams, Arachchis, Kanganis—should dress. Only Vellala (Goyigama) headmen, who constituted the highest caste, in the Sinhalese hierarchy were entitled to wear a costume made of velvet adorned with gold buttons and loops. Mudaliyars of other castes had to be content with silk and silver buttons. Similar gradations were visible in the description of the sword and belt of headmen of different castes.[30]

The Juta[31]

Under the column 'Footwear' in the Gazette notification of 1935 appeared the term *'Juta'*. Jutas, a Telugu term, were specified as 'the only authorised shoes and when worn they should be worn with white socks'. Early twentieth-century photographs of Kandyan chiefs in their ceremonial dress suggest that the jutas were shoes similar to what a Nilame wears today: velvet black or red shoes decorated with flowers sewn in golden thread. The shoe is pointed, the tip is a ball which goes up slightly and the heel is low. Although shoes were not commonly worn in Ceylon there is evidence of other types of shoes being worn: the jutas were not the only shoes that the British could have officialised in their Gazette. Indeed even among the royalty, quite different shoes were worn as late as the seventeenth century. The shoes of King Rajasinha II were described thus by some Germans who worked for the Dutch East India Company:

> The King dresseth himself as he pleases ... His shoes are only leathern soles with strings, one of which comes up between his toes and the other two or three come around his foot and tie the sole fast to it: and all these straps are set out with sapphires and rubies.

In the Low-Country Orientalist travellers have written about the customs of the Sinhalese. Robert Percival describing the dress of a Mudaliyar mentions his shoes very briefly: 'On their feet they have a kind of sandal but commonly go bare legged.'[32] James Cordiner in 1807 is more descriptive:

> In common with all the other natives of India, their legs are bare, stockings never being used; but they wear a kind of slippers made of red leather ornamented with gold leaf, having the heel folded down and the sharp pointed toe turned up ... On entering a house they leave them. Women wear 'slippers of red and white leather.'[33]

The Telugu name 'Juta' for the Kandyan shoe and its appearance during the reign of the Nayakkar kings seems to point towards a recent South Indian origin. But not only did the British consolidate the juta as the only authentic shoe, they also vested it with added features: the juta was transformed into the oriental shoe par excellence. Indeed it is interesting to note that in the Gazette of 1935 jutas are recommended not only for the Kandyan Sinhalese but also for Muslim and Tamil officials if they choose to wear a sarong instead of trousers. For a Ceylon Tamil the recommended uniform gives the following details:

> With sarong: if shoes are worn, jutas without socks or shoes with socks and matching stockings.[34]

This is followed by the important recommendation that 'jutas must be taken off in the presence of the Governor.[35]

So the juta lost first its South Indian character, then its regional/Kandyan character, and reinvented by the colonial administrator, became the oriental shoe worn by Kandyans, Muslims and Tamils. It also was coded as a sartorial symbol of subjugation: its presence on the foot of a native official in the presence of the Governor was considered an affront. British colonial policy on official footwear clearly shows their attempt to subsume the complexities of Sri Lankan cultures under the unifying idea of the Orient. It also shows that Kandyans could remain pure even as they wore south Indian jutas on their feet.

Twentieth-Century Impressions of Ceylon

Apart from the censuses that contributed to drawing clear-cut boundaries between groups, there were other colonial writings which documented the 'authentic' in society as the British envisioned it. Among these, the *Twentieth-Century Impressions of Ceylon* stands out. The explicit purpose of this volume was clearly defined in the preface. It was 'to give a perfect microcosm of the colony or dependency treated'. It was 'the outcome of an enterprise designed to give in an attractive form, full and reliable information with reference to the outlying parts of the Empire.[36] What this book did in fact was to chart the 'authentic' in Ceylonese society or what was worth while museumising. In this operation the objects of the inquiry, namely the leading families in Ceylonese society became willing subjects.

The book is composed of a number of essays and illustrated with black and white photographs of men and women who belong to the traditional or the new elite. It purports to reach completeness and accuracy.

The photographs give a rational and ordered version of the diverse dress of the Sinhalese, Tamil and Muslim people. No judgment or opinion is offered. The description is purely informative. In the same way, the costumes are timeless, unanchored, dehistoricised. When one sifts through this photograph album of solemn faces in their best costumes what is conveyed is the author's mitigated respect for his subjects wrapped either in their authentic dress or dressed in the most fashionable western outfit. The violence of the colonial gaze is absent, replaced with the inquiring search for the traditional and the elegant.

Two pages of text in this book/photograph album of four hundred pages are devoted to the dress of the Sinhalese. In these, clear distinctions are made between on the one hand the dress of the Low-Country Sinhalese and the Kandyans and on the other that of the lower classes and upper classes. The Low-Country Sinhalese man's ordinary wear is described thus:

> ... a white or coloured cloth called the 'comboy', folded around the lower part of the body and depending below the knee more or less, according to the caste of the wearer. [The] better orders assume the European coat either of modern cut or of the old pattern with gold buttons and gold worked button holes and sometimes the comboy over the trouser ... . The highest rank among them is the Mudaliyar. It is either borne ex-officio or is conferred by the Governor as an honorary distinction. On state occasions the Mudaliyars attend Government House in full costume, when they wear handsomely ornamented curved dirks, suspended from the shoulder by richly worked gold belts. Some of them wear around their necks golden

medals of considerable size, bearing an inscription commemorative of the services rendered to government by the wearer or their ancestors on account of which the medal was presented to them'.

The Sinhalese women generally wear a short jacket and a comboy, and secure their long and glossy hair with gold or silver pins and sometimes a small prettily worked comb. No covering for the head is used. The wealthier wear European costume and a profusion of jewellery when they go abroad.

The ordinary dress of the Kandyans is:

a cloth round the loins. They never wear the comb and their beards are allowed to grow. Their chiefs envelop themselves in an immense quantity of muslin wound again and again round the waist and allowed to fall in folds to the ankle. When in full dress they wear a jacket with a white gigote shaped hat, somewhat resembling two saucers laid one onto the other with the rim meeting, made either of white or black cloth and ornamented with silver or gold. The dress of the women consists of a cloth which they fold after the fashion of Hindu women, gracefully about them. Their hair is tied in a knot hanging down rather low at the back of the head and they are fond of jewellery.[37]

For the writer of these lines—exemplifying the colonial mind—the Low-Country Mudaliyar, who on occasions 'assumed the European coat' and wore medals given to him by the colonial state, embodied modernity while his Kandyan counterpart remained firmly entrenched in the traditional realm. The Low-Country man's costume was described as a mixture of East and West. The Kandyan costume which seemingly drew only from indigenous culture was perceived as being more 'authentic'.

Communal Constructions of Authenticity

When the Commission on constitutional reform headed by Lord Donoughmore which remained in Ceylon from

13 November 1927 to 18 January 1928 called for representations by groups and individuals, the political landscape of the country changed. A new type of politics which is best described as the politics of identity emerged.

Thirty-four sittings were held for the purpose of taking evidence and 140 witnesses and delegations were examined.[38] The arrival of the Commission had the effect of stimulating political activity in the island. Ethnicity imposed itself as a viable strategy to secure more advantages in the new constitution. The authenticity of their own ethnic group or race was claimed by many elite leaders who used the imagery of purity, lineage and distinctiveness to ascertain their place in society.

A delegation claiming to represent the 32,000 Burghers scattered over the leading towns, appeared before the Commission. The main point they made was the distinctiveness of the Burghers vis-à-vis Eurasians and other people of mixed descent. The Dutch Burgher Union of Ceylon formed in 1908 aimed at promoting a distinctively Dutch Burgher ethnic identity among the middle-class Burghers of Colombo and purging the outsiders, mainly the Portuguese Burghers. The latter commonly referred to as mechanics or *tupasses*, by the very nature of their occupations—did not earn the right to call themselves Burghers. The Burghers constructed their authenticity by defining strict laws based on lineage.[39]

Similarly the Malays of Ceylon who numbered 15,000 used a racial argument to demarcate themselves from the larger Muslim community. In the mid-nineteenth century the British administration had found it convenient to bring together the small communities of Ceylon—Moors, Malays, Afghans, Bohras and Memons—under the umbrella term Muslim. The Malays on the basis of a proclaimed Javanese identity wanted separate political representation.[40]

At the Donoughmore sittings authenticity became a pliable instrument used by all small communities that feared that they would lose their place in society if the law of numbers were to prevail. The etiquette of authenticity followed by the smaller groups was very similar to that displayed by the Sinhala nationalists.

Malays would distinguish themselves from Moors by not wearing the red felt fez but tying a cloth around their head.

The fez was a significant community symbol for the Moors. In 1906 Mr Abdul Cader, a prominent Moor, resisted the Chief Justice's order forbidding him to appear in court with both head and feet covered. A meeting of 30,000 persons in support of him was held in Maradana.[41]

Dress was an important component in identity display. Jaffna Tamils who wore the cloth undivided just like the Sinhalese, wore the turban as a sign of separateness from the major community. The definition of the authentic self by various communities rarely entered into conflict with the colonial constructions of communities. It was indeed within the social framework sketched by the colonial minds that communities reinvented signs of identity and difference.

Gendering Authenticity

The Ceylonese experience shows that through their participation in the constructing of authenticities for various communities in the island, the British conceptualised the difference between Great Britain and the East in terms not only of history and race, but also gender.

Men with Combs: Masculinising Men

Colonial rule had elaborated a system where people belonged somewhere with certainty, and proof of this belonging was visible. Cross-gender behaviour was therefore troubling to European men, accustomed to a clear demarcation of gender roles and appearance. For these reasons the *konde* (hair tied up in a bun) of southern Sinhalese men caused much worry to them. Why would self-respecting men keep their hair long and worse, tie it up in a bun over which a comb was fixed?

As late as in 1887, in spite of the increase in commoditisation, men were killing themselves over the right of certain people to wear the comb. Men from an elite Oli family from south of Colombo planned to attend a marriage ceremony wearing combs in the Goyigama (traditionally highest caste) style. The local Goyigamas successfully prevented them from doing so and an Oli was killed in the affray. The Governor Arthur Gordon opposed taking any action against them for he believed that the Olis had provoked the riot by giving 'grievous offence'.[42]

The operation of cutting off the konde, which became a quasi-obsession for the colonial rulers, was an integral part of the silent violence of colonial rule. To be fair, impressions of the konde was mixed among the British but most would have approved the 1906 ruling according to which the colonial state specified that volunteers in Ceylon may no longer wear a konde. This new law would affect thirty Sinhalese men. Until then long hair had not been considered a threat. The editors of the *Ceylon National Review* a mildly radical magazine sarcastically commented:

> We suppose it interferes in some mysterious way with the defence of the Empire, still can't help wonder how.

They suggested these men should retire from service rather than comply.[43]

In European culture cutting the hair of one's enemy signifies total submission. Historical examples are many: from Julius Caesar who cut the long hair of the Gaul chiefs to the scalping and eventual decimation of native Americans. For British rulers in Ceylon, was the sight of long-haired men was a threat to their power?

Foucauldian notions of 'bio-power' and 'the body surface' offers some powerful tools for interrogating colonial visions of the body. In his later works, Foucault identifies a distinctive mode of modern power that produces its effects from within the sphere of the self—through regulation, inhibitions and introspection—a mode that he calls bio-power. Accounts of the functioning of bio-power have all involved institutions and practices concerned with the regulation and 'inscription' of bodies—such as medicine, punishment and sexuality. In Ceylon, district courts had the power to inflict punishment of up to one year in prison, fifty lashes, a fine of one hundred pounds or any of the two above. There was no formal limit to the punishment which the Supreme Court could impose, though in practice the death sentence was passed only in cases of murder. The 1880s reforms led to a reduction of lashes to 25. But this was reversed in the 1890s when magistrates were given the power to order corporal punishment for specific offenses.

> Whippings in Sri Lanka were carried out with a cat-o-nine-tails and flayed the back of the prisoner scarring him for life.[44]

Doing away with the konde was a central part of the strengthening of colonial bio-power.

The violence against natives was subtly evoked by Denham who saw the process of colonialism as the inevitable march of progress and modernity. His approach was not different from that of another modernist: Anagarika Dharmapala urged his countrymen not to wear combs on the head 'like Batavian Malays'.[45] Denham was less forceful when he remarked:

> Another change which is taking place is in the wearing of the hair. At one time there were signs that combs were going out of fashion and this distinctive mark of the Low-Country Sinhalese—the crescent-shaped semi-circular tortoise-shell comb worn on the head seemed likely to become obsolete. In the village, however there has been little change and it is only amongst the young men in the towns that the comb is no longer seen, though the large tortoise-shell comb worn at the back of the head is rarely used. The knot of hair tied behind—the konde—is undoubtedly less frequently seen and the fashion of wearing the hair short is now popular.[46]

What E.B. Denham called a 'distinctive mark of the Low-Country Sinhalese' was according to popular tales, introduced in the eighteenth century by a Malay prince who was deported from Java to Ceylon by the Dutch. Popular stories claim that the custom of wearing a comb came after a Dutch Governor had suggested to a native chief that a comb would keep his hair turned up in place. From then on headwear (hats) was no longer used among the Low-Country Sinhalese who adopted the comb. The comb became part of 'tradition'. Other accounts trace the origin of the comb to antiquity. De Alwis cited Sullivan in *The Bungalow and Tent*:

> So dearly do the Cinghalese prize the fashion of wearing high combs that the tyranny of the Tamil kings could devise no more

galling and offensive enaction against the liberty and predilections of their Low-Country subjects than by forbidding the use of that article.

De Alwis regrets though that he is unable to identify the edict which could have been passed any time between 203 B.C. when Elara ruled to 1023 A.D. when Mahinda IV was carried captive to the court of India.[47] More than the veracity of the dates what is significant is De Alwis's own interest in the subject in the 1920s and his attempt to communalise the story of the comb.

Perhaps what unnerved the colonial rulers of Ceylon about the comb even more than the turban in India was its feminine character. By wearing combs, Sinhalese men were in effect becoming women. An interesting account of the feminine character attributed to Sinhalese men can be found in a popular novel written in 1926 by Francois de Croisset, *La Feerie Cinghalaise*. An American character in the novel summarises the general idea:

> What a naughty little habit men have here to comb their hair and dress as women do.[48]

This unpretentious novel tells us more about French prejudices and British attitudes than about Sinhalese customs. In fact although the novel is set in Colombo, Anuradhapura and Kandy there are hardly any encounters with natives. The few references to natives reveal however a very specious understanding of Sinhalese society. An underlying theme is the long hair of the Sinhalese men, their wearing of a comb, and their sexually feminine and provocative characteristics such as long eyelashes, oily bodies, nudity:

> A young Sinhalese man, with girlish hair, naked under a sarong that sweat placates to his back.[49]

A waiter is described thus:

> In white dress, his oiled hair kept up by a forked comb, a boy sculptured in a brown nut, whose eyelashes seem false ... [F]eline servants who have long shiny hair put up by a comb made of shell.[50]

Sinhalese men were described as feline but not muscular. In this way they differed from the 'more muscular Tamils'.[51]

The effeminacy of Sinhalese men was part of the general appreciation of men from India by British rulers. As early as in 1750s, Robert Orme spoke of the effeminacy of the inhabitants of Hindustan. Gender in fact helped define the contrast between ruler and ruled and provided a way to order Britain's relations with its Indian and Ceylonese subjects. According to the powerful domestic ideology which grew in Britain in the early nineteenth century, innate and demonstrable biological traits defined a fundamental difference between male and female. By their very nature women were fragile, passive, and emotional, in contrast to men who were held to be strong, active and intellectual. These differences in the structuring of the body, in turn, dictated differing patterns of behaviour for men and women. Men were to be active in the public world, competing against each other for power and wealth; women, from the sanctuary of the home, were to nurture their husbands and children.[52]

The very nature of British imperial experience brought into prominence the 'masculine' virtues—such as control and self-discipline, and de-emphasised the 'feminine' virtues such as tenderness and feeling which were expressive of the softer side of human nature.[53]

Sinhalese men were considered feminine just as were men belonging to particular communities in India such as Bengalis. But where the Bengali and Sinhalese situation differed was that not only were men considered feminine by colonial observers in Ceylon, Sinhalese women were attributed masculine features.

The Myth of the Graceful Oriental Woman

Many Europeans arriving the colonial worlds of the nineteenth century were interested in the sensual, physical, and bodily nature of indigenous cultures and the early ethnographic texts that often framed their interest in these subjects shared this preoccupation. Nineteenth-century travel narratives about Ceylon define a very specific conceptual domain. Among the more negative features highlighted by colonial minds were the absence of good looks among women. Nineteenth-century writers also stressed the premature ageing of women. Knox had commented in the late seventeenth century in a positive manner about the freedom enjoyed by women:

> The men are not jealous of their wives, for the greatest ladies in the land will frequently talk and discourse with any men they please although their husbands be in presence.[54]

But, in the nineteenth century, the prevalent view, as summed up by a British colonel in *La Feerie Cinghalaise* was.

> Strange country ... everything is nice, except the women. At twenty, they are finished.[55]

Sinhalese women, it seemed troubled colonial minds as Kerala women did. They did not conform to the idea which prevailed in the Raj of the oriental woman as mysterious, beautiful but tragic, feeble and in need of protection. By challenging the traditional understanding of the relationship between anatomy and social roles, Sinhalese women created a feeling of uneasiness. Hence, the cruel indictment of the colonial.

The perceived effeminacy of the Sinhala man and the masculine features of the women were linked to their attire too:

> The only visible distinction between the sexes consists in the women wearing rather shorter jackets than the men, enjoying generally rather coarser features, and dispensing with the masculine appendages of combs and parasols.[56]

Captain Percival stated that women 'get old and haggard in their looks immediately after they pass twenty' while Reverend James Cordiner declaimed that: 'The women are lower in stature than the men and the greater part of them are not comely.'[57] According to Elisabeth Harris, Sri Lanka women were neither romanticised nor praised by British men[58] one of the reasons being that their dress was perceived as unbecoming.

Cordiner in 1807 described women's dress:

> The pieces of cloth worn by the women of the lower order
> are longer than those of the men, reaching generally below the
> knee: and the greater part of them have the addition of little
> white shifts, like short jackets, just long enough to cover their
> breasts. Others throw a piece of coarse cloth loosely over their
> shoulders to answer the same purpose. But several of the lower
> castes are not permitted the use of any of these privileges and
> are obliged to appear in public and perform their ordinary
> labour with their bosoms completely exposed. Cruel and
> indelicate as their custom appears no individual can transgress
> it with impunity.[59]

92

Dress was sometimes seen as inadequate, sometimes as
simply plain. It lacked the exuberance colonial minds expected
from oriental women.

> The dress of the women in the higher stations is of the same
> form as that of the poorer sort but their clothes are finer, and
> a greater quantity is worn. The dress that is used in the form
> of a petticoat is often of coloured silk, or satin over which is
> thrown white muslin embroidered with flowers and spangled
> with gold. The shift which is always the upper garment, is
> trimmed round the bottom with lace, and decorated at the
> sleeves with ruffles of the same materials.[60]

On the whole the variety in the looks of the Sri Lankan
woman and the simplicity of their attire puzzled the western
male who was looking for some idealised oriental women.
Construing an authentic Sinhalese woman was therefore of
no interest to colonial writers and officials. In sharp contrast
to their role in gelling male identities through official
costumes colonialism had little impact on the formation of
'authentic women' of different communities. Official Ceylon
just as official India did not concern itself with women's
attire. Colonial minds found more resources in the willing
group of men, chiefs and aspiring leaders whose claims to
authenticity had, in their understanding, more grounds to
support.

Conclusion

Authenticity as it was articulated by colonial minds and gradually accepted by the colonised was firmly steeped in the ceremonial, while the elements of authenticity in day-to-day life were purged: hence the rejection of the comb of the Low-Country as an emblem and the display of infinite respect for men dressed in ceremonial clothes such as Mudaliyar costumes. A particular feature of the modernity brought about with colonialism was the way in which 'oriental costumes' were relegated to the ceremonial domain while in the day-to-day existence of Ceylonese, western clothes were adopted with the stamp of approval of the colonial masters. Just as in countries such as France, regional costumes became part of the folk culture through the uniformising policies of the Third Republic, in Ceylon, 'native' costumes were expected to be worn only on special occasions.

93

Authenticity in women was never an issue as they rarely entered the public or ceremonial sphere. Authenticity was not the prerogative of the Sinhalese as each ethnic group/race articulated its own authenticity and was in British eyes, the repository of a specific authenticity in the ceremonial sphere. Colonialism was made possible and then sustained and strengthened as much by cultural technologies of rule as it was by the more obvious and brutal modes of conquest. The gaze that colonisers deployed upon the people they ruled, their enumerative technologies, their descriptive divides were an important part of the project of exercising power efficiently. Arguably the ways in which dress was imagined—authentic, masculine, feminine—by the colonial minds helped in the colonial project of control and command over the colonised body.

NOTES

1. Fernand Braudel. *The Identity of France:* Vol. I. New York: Harper and Row. 1988: 23.
2. Benedict Anderson. *The Spectre of Comparisons: Nationalism, South-East Asia and the World.* London: Verso. 1998: 36.

3. Robert Percival. *An Account of the Island of Ceylon*. 1803: 114–15.

4. Report of the Mission of Ceylon by Fr Antonio Pereira in V. Perniola. *The Catholic Church in Sri Lanka: The Dutch Period*. Vol. II, 1712–46. Dehiwela: Tisara Press 1983: 502–04.

5. B. Anderson. *Imagined Communities*. London: Verso: XIV. See also David N. Lorenzen's excellent critique of the constructivist point of view in 'Who Invented Hinduism'. *Comparative Studies in Society and History*. 41: 4 October 1999: 630–59.

6. B.S. Cohn. 'The Census, Social Structure and Objectification in South Asia'. In B.S. Cohn (ed.) *An Anthropologist Among the Historians and Other Essays*. New Delhi: Oxford University Press, 1990: 232.

7. Cited in N.K. Sarkar. *The Demography of Ceylon*. Colombo: 1957: 19.

8. N.K. Sarkar. *Op.cit.*: 18–20.

9. E.B. Denham. *Ceylon at the Census of 1911*. Colombo, 1912: 11.

10. N.K. Sarkar. *Op.cit.*: 19.

11. *Ibid.*

12. Census of the Island of Ceylon 1871, General Report. Colombo, 1873: IX–XI.

13. R.S. Smith. 'Rule by Records and Rule by Reports: Complementary Aspects of the British Imperial Rule by Law'. In Veena Das (ed.), *The Word and the World*. New Delhi: Sage. 1986: 153–54.

14. B. Ryan. *Caste in Modern Ceylon*. New Brunswick, Rutgers University Press, 1953: 19. He gives the following definition of caste: a social organisation structure functioning through hierarchial birth status groups, they or their sub-units being communalistic and usually endogamous, and possessing functional or ritual roles, including symbolic expressions of social distance and privilege in reference to and in distinction from other social groups in the great society.

15. The term 'Moors' is derived from 'Maurs', used by the Portuguese to refer to the Muslims of Mauritania. All Muslims except the Malays in Ceylon came to be referred to by this term. The term 'Malabars', initially employed for the inhabitants of the Malabar coast, became part of the vocabulary of the European powers to describe all Tamils in Ceylon.

16. *Return of the Population of the Maritime Districts of the Island of Ceylon*. Colombo, 1816: 24. Co 59/29, *Census of Ceylon 1824*.

17. E.B. Denham. *Op.cit.*: 177.

18. E.B. Denham. *Op.cit.*: 11.
19. Census of the Island of Ceylon, 1871, General Report. Colombo, 1873; Census of Ceylon 1881, General Report and Statements and Tables. Colombo, 1882.
20. E.B. Denham. *Op.cit.*: 194.
21. *Ibid.*: 209.
22. R.A.L.H. Gunawardena. 'The People of the Lion. The Sinhala Identity and Ideology in History and Historiography'. *Sri Lanka Journal of Humanities*. 5: 1 & 2, 1979: 30–31.

23. A.J. Wilson. *The Break-Up of Sri Lanka. The Sinhalese-Tamil Conflict*. C.Hurst, London: 1988: 28.
24. E.B. Denham. *Op.cit.*: 177.
25. B.S. Cohn. 'Representing Authority in Victorian India'. In E. Hobsbawn and T. Ranger (eds.), *The Invention of Tradition*. Cambridge: Cambridge University Press: 182.
26. D.A. Kotelawela, 'Some Aspects of Social Change in the South-East of Sri Lanka *c.* 1700–1833'. *Social Science Review: Studies in the Social History of Sri Lanka*, 1987: 75.
27. Schedule X in CO54/124 in M. Roberts. *Op.cit.*: 94.
28. Ceylon Government Gazette, 17 April 1935, No. 8.116.
29. Co54/960/12, Letter from first and second Adigars and Diiyawardana Nilame of Ceylon to Governor Caldecott, 12 September 1938.
30. Ceylon Almanac and Compendium of Useful information 1821.
31. See Appendix for details of the Gazette notification.
32. Robert Percival. *An Account of the Island of Ceylon*, 1803. Asian Educational Services, New Delhi 1990.
33. James Cordiner. *Description of Ceylon Containing an Account of the Country. Inhabitants and Natural Productions: 1807* Vol. 1. Tisara Prakasakayo, Dehiwela: 1983.
34. Ceylon Government Casette, 1935.
35. *Ibid.*
36. A. Wright (ed.). *Twentieth-Century Impressions of Ceylon*. London, Lloyd's Greater Britain Publishing Co, 1907.
37. *Ibid.*: 334–35.
38. Command Papers 3131, Ceylon. Report of the Special Commission on the Constitution of Ceylon, July 1928: 11–12.
39. R.G. Anthonisz. *The Burghers of Ceylon*. Colombo. 1927: 5; 'The Dutch Burgher Union of Ceylon'. *Journal of the Dutch Burgher Union of Ceylon*, 1, 1908; 'The Constitution and By-laws of the Dutch Burgher Union of Ceylon', *J.D.B.U.C.*, 1, 1908: 52–60.

40. Nathan Mss 602, Evidence of the Malay Political Association, 23 November 1927.

41. *The Ceylon National Review*, No. 1, January 1906: 89.

42. John D. Rogers. *Crime, Justice and Society in Colonial Sri Lanka*. London, Curzon Press, 1987: 171.

43. *The Ceylon National Review*, No.1, January 1906: 97.

44. John Rogers. *Op.cit.*: 44.

45. A Guruge (ed.). *Anagarika Dharmapala: Return to Righteousness*. Colombo: Government Press, 1965: 509.

46. E.B. Denham. *Op.cit.*: 172.

47. A. Alwis. 'Combs. Uses and Users', *C.A.L.R.*, 6 (2) October, 1920: 100–101.

48. F.de Croisset. *La Feerie Cinghalaise. Ceylan avec les Anglais*. Paris, 1926: 39.

49. *Ibid.*: 34.

50. *Ibid.*: 37–39.

51. *Ibid.*: 44.

52. T.R. Metcalf. *Ideologies of the Raj*, The New Cambridge History of India, III, 4. Cambridge: Cambridge University Press. 1994: 92–94.

53. Ashis Nandy. *The Intimate Enemy: Loss and Recovery of Self under Colonialism*. New Delhi: Oxford University Press. 1984: 31–34.

54. R. Knox. *An Historical Relation of Ceylon*. Dehiwela, Tisara Press. 1958: 123–24. (This book was first published in 1681.)

55. F. de Croisset. *Op.cit.*: 54.

56. E. Sullivan. *The Bungalow and the Tent or A Visit to Ceylon*. London: Richard Bentley. 1854: 19. Cited in E. Harris. *The Gaze of the Colonisers: British Views of Local Women in Nineteenth Century Sri Lanka*, SSA: 1994.

57. R. Percival. *An Account of the Island of Ceylon*. London: C. & R. Baldwin. 1803: 181; J. Cordiner. *A Description of Ceylon*. Vol. I. London: Longman, Rees and Orme: 1807: 94.

58. E. Harris. *Op.cit.*

59. J. Cordiner. *Op.cit.* Vol. I.

60. J. Cordiner. *Op.cit.* Vol. I: 105.

Chapter Five

DRESS AND MEMORY:
A DRAUGHTSMAN'S STORY

My great-grandfather lives through three photographs. Each
one tells me a different story of a man who fought, worked
and complied. It is the same man in these three pictures but
in each he wears a different dress and a different face.

This paper is about the multiplicity of the self of Wahala
Tantrige Don Alphonsus Maria de Ligouri Ranaweerasinghe
Perera (DAL) who did not write his memoirs and whose
letters are lost or destroyed. All that is left are these
photographs and his line drawings, mute records of archaeology,
an account of his work at Medirigiriya, many plans and paintings, passing hints in the mediated writings of his superior

H.C.P. Bell about their work together, and a few memories. In this sense these black and white photographs are unique clues, a kind of involuntary memory in which things once forgotten are randomly recalled by images and where the self of DAL is demultiplied.

There is a frozen arrested quality to the photograph. As Roland Barthes puts it, the photograph, unlike other systems of representation, can never deny the existence of the referent of the lost object. In this sense the photograph never ceases in its attempt to restore the lost object, the referent that has been but is no longer.[1] DAL's clothes speak to me, tell of an everyday existence, forge connections with a social and affective life. With them I can pull a few strings together, comb dry government reports and technical writings, and, building from chance and fragmentary materials, weave a half-imaginary life.

Since the self that is represented in the photograph is a self that is staged in the setting of the studio or by the photographer's reading of his subject, it is worth taking a detour to look at photography at the turn of the century.

Photography as Family Archive

Invented in 1836, photography was brought to Ceylon by foreign travellers and administrators. Natives were photographed as exotic subjects and their images adorned books which described the strange lands outside Europe. Photographs were later adopted by the natives who had few qualms about their image being captured inside a small black box. But while Buddhist practice never condemned the representation of human beings—wall paintings in temples of kings and ordinary people were common—the habit of hanging pictorial representations of ancestors in one's house, hut or palace was a new act.

There were many different types of studios, those for the Europeans, those for the natives, those for the richer segments of the westernised classes. European photographers in Ceylon first catered to a purely European clientele eager to immortalise their families at various stages in their life.

Plate Limited, a well-known Studio was established in 1890 and became the agent for Kodak films and accessories.

From 1889 Sinhala newspapers carried advertisements for photographic studios offering photographs on location for those who were not able to come to the studio.[2] By the 1920s studios were found even in remote areas such as Nawalapitiya.[3] Clearly photography had ceased to be the preserve of elite groups and was becoming a necessary item for everyone. In 1916 Plate offered a prize of the value of 15 rupees for an amateur photograph developed and printed in any of its studios in Nuwara Eliya, Kandy or Colombo. Photography was graduating from being a necessity to becoming a hobby. In the 1930s it became an art.

'A portrait by Plate Limited is the acme of photographic art' read an advertisement from the 1930s.[4]

The wedding photograph was most probably the first occasion when natives visited the studio and were confronted with the ritual of self-representation. They stood or sat in their best attire taking up the role that they assumed was theirs or the role that the photographer master-of-ceremonies gave them. Often the husband stood towering over his seated wife. The access to a new mode of representation would have increased the sense of self-importance and democratised the desire for a social statement. Photographers understood this need and inside the studios as in a theatre—through accessories, columns, curtains—it was the entire stature of a person that was represented. Gestures, attitudes were staged: photographers became masters of the pose. The pose in which people attempted to make their faces and postures conform to certain post-medieval European painting conventions was the same in every corner of the globe. Later each important event in the life of the family from birth to graduation entered the family album which became the repositor of the passing of time. Death, though, was not recorded even in this society which had few taboos about death.

The importance of the photo album in European societies has been highlighted by the works of many social historians who have shown the democratisation of the gallery of portraits, once the privilege of kings and queens or people of some means and social standing. Soon each family had its own portraits. To photograph one's children was to become the historiographer of childhood and to prepare for them as a kind of legacy the image of what they had been. The photo album expressed the truth of the social souvenir. New members in the family were subjected to photography as a ritual of integration. Social memory was made of those events that were included in the album. The images of the past arranged in a chronological fashion helped forge or strengthen ties of community.[5]

In a way, photography shattered memory by multiplying and democratising it. It brought a precision, a 'truth' in visual memory which had never existed before. It allowed people to keep within them a memory of time and of chronological evolution. But the truth of the photograph could be a doctored truth. From the 1860s, photographs could be touched up. In Europe certain traits of the face which were considered less attractive were erased: scars and pimples disappeared giving way to clear, smooth faces. In colonial Ceylon the faces of the natives were often lightened for fair was considered beautiful and the sign of higher status in a country where the working classes were constantly subjected to the burning rays of the sun. Photography brought new norms of beauty to the most remote areas and paid tribute to post-medieval European conventions of beauty.

History as Memory

Recreating the life of a man who was born nearly one hundred years before me is a tenuous enterprise because between the present and the past there is a no obvious road to follow. While traditional history was literally built on the idea of a continuity between past and present, and the idea that the past can throw light on the present, today this relationship is well and truly broken. History is today based on the conscience of a radical break and of the obstacles that must be overcome in order to abolish it. Many historians believe that the historian has a mission which is to resonate the voice of the actors of the past and show their countryside with its colour and exoticism.[6]

But is the past of nineteenth century and early twentieth century Ceylon more intelligible to us than thirteenth century France? Perhaps not. 'It's not so long ago—people remember this period', I have often been told. Some witnesses are still alive. The historian only needs to record their testimony. But memory is sometimes the prime suspect and as Pierre Nora has shown, memory and history are opposed in many ways:

> Memory is life, always taken on by living groups and thus she is in permanent evolution, open to the dialectic of souvenir and amnesia, unconscious of successive deformations, vulnerable to all uses and manipulations, susceptible to long periods of inactivity and sudden revitalisations. History is the reconstruction, always problematic and incomplete, of what is not there. Because she is affective and magical, memory accommodates herself only of details that comfort her: she feeds on vague souvenirs, telescoping, global or floating, particular or symbolic. History because it is an intellectual operation calls for analysis and critical discourse ... At the heart of history is a critique of spontaneous memory. The true mission of history is to destroy and delegitimate the lived past.[7]

So in many ways making history is to liberate oneself from memory, put one's souvenirs in order, put them into chains and regularities, explain and understand, transform an affective and emotional lived moment into a thought.

The Year of DAL's Birth, 1869

On an old notebook my maternal grandmother jotted down our family histories: births, deaths, names in full were carefully inscribed in her shaky handwriting. From a page of this book I know DAL was born on 2 August 1869 in his ancestral home in Kotte. He descended from the Wasala Mudiyanse of the Kotte Kingdom which went back as far as Don Juan Dharmapala, King of Kotte in the mid-sixteenth century, and Dona Catherina.

Was it a sunny morning or not, who knows. A newspaper weather report says the temperature in Colombo was 32° and the direction of the wind W–SW. While Galle was subject to light winds and clouds, Jaffna was calm and rainy. On 2 August 1869, G.E. Jansz named his firm Albert Jansz and Co.[8] That month, horse races were held in Colombo and a pound of good white rice cost Rs 67½. That year was an eventful year, as every year, every month, every day is. Colombo's serious and scholarly minded readers were able to buy and read the *First Book of the Hitopadesa* with interlinear translation by Professor Max Muller, the more distracted lot enjoyed the *Arabian Nights*, trembled at De Foe's *History of the Devil* and learnt the art of love in the *Etiquette of Love Courtship*.[9] The Saturday issue of the *Ceylon Observer* commenced in the beginning of 1869. The telegraph to Jaffna was completed in May of that year and the Suez Canal opened a few months later breaking the isolation of regions and countries, drawing them into vaster networks and imagined relations. In Colombo the demolition of the walls of the Fort commenced with the blowing up of the Rotterdam Best, while the erection of a Lighthouse on the great Basses Rocks commenced. That year, *hemleia vastratix*, a devastating leaf disease, struck the coffee plantations and spread quickly through the plantation district destroying the coffee industry within fifteen years. On the last day of the year the *Kandy Herald* newspaper collapsed.[10]

While DAL was growing up in a Catholic family, the Buddhist revival was gathering momentum. Not surprisingly he was sent to St Benedict's College in Kotahena, a district of Colombo that was then a multi-cultural and multi-religious area. At least half of the residents of Kotahena were Christians and one-quarter Buddhists. But in the second half of the nineteenth century it was the centre of the revivalist activities of Mohotivatte Gunananda, a monk who presided over the temple of Dipaduttamaramaya for over fifty years. Revivalism began as a phenomenon precipitated by the institutional reform of the *Sangha*, the Buddhist order of monks. Initially the revivalist impulse emerged from a malaise in the Sangha due to an interruption of the higher ordination (*upasampada*) of the monks who comprised it. In the early nineteenth century, candidates from certain disadvantaged castes began to seek and in fact received ordination, rather than the highland Goyigama of the Siyam Fraternity alone, as had so far been the case. A new era was beginning for Sinhalese Buddhism with the birth of new fraternities such as the Amarapura Nikaya and the Kalyanivansa founded by Maligaspa Mangala of the Raja Mahavihara at Kotte.

Twenty years before DAL's birth, *dharmasabhas* (societies for the protection of the Dhamma) were organised at Kotte. As a child DAL would have felt the tremors of a renewed Buddhist religion. To strengthen his Christian faith perhaps he was sent to school in Kotahena. Kotahena had in 1881 a population of 26,692. Colombo was then a predominantly non-Buddhist city. The largest church in Colombo, St Lucia Cathedral, which the Roman Catholics completed in 1910 after 34 years of construction, stood firmly in Kotahena. The nineteenth century also saw, as a response to a renascent Buddhism, a mushrooming of Christian centres of learning. The boys school in Kotahena known as St Benedicts was ready for occupation in 1865. The Convent for the Sisters of Good Shepherd was completed a few years later in 1867. This is where DAL spent his formative years, taught by Catholic priests to read, write and pray. In the early twentieth century, St Benedicts was described as 'the largest and most preogressive school in the colony which gives education to more than 1,000 boys and is conducted by the Christian Brothers—the devoted sons of St John Baptist de la Salle'.[11] The principal failing of the college was that the tuition it provided was 'sufficient for an ordinary commercial and clerical training', but did not cater to the higher educational needs of the rising indigenous middle class. The later creation of St Joseph's college would fulfil this pressing need.

After that we lose track of DAL until he joined the Archaeological Survey in 1890 at the age of 21. There, DAL took part in a small way in the recovery of ruins and participated in the mapping of the past, drawing lost cities with his enchanted pencil and pulling them out of their torpor.

It was while DAL was growing up in Kotte, that people began to learn oriental languages and to translate classical texts. The first thirty chapters of the *Mahavamsa* or *Great Chronicle*, which runs from 500 B.C. to the time of the British occupation, had already been translated from the Pali by George Turner in 1837. The *Chronicle* was originally written in classical Pali verse on ola leaves and deposited in temple libraries. A monk called Galle Unanse, convinced that a *taika* or prose explanation of these verses existed, searched for such a manuscript together with the young government agent George Turner. They eventually discovered the taika in 1826 in an ancient temple at Mulkirigala near Walasmulla. Turner translated the *Mahavamsa* into English and nearly fifty years later Sri Sumangala and Batuwan Tudawe translated it into Sinhalese. The translation of the *Mahavamsa* was a turning point. With this achievement began the operation by which experts decided what should be secured in a museum made of brick and stone where the heritage of the Sinhalese would be stored for posterity. From then on, too, the government recognised their responsibility for all aspects of archaeological activity. It was felt that they had a duty to recover the past and exhibit it. The Archaeological Commission was set up by the Governor, Sir Hercules Robinson as early as in 1868 with the sole purpose of collecting inscriptions for the Museum.

Colonial administrators ventured to the remotest corners of the island—through submerged fields and thick forests—to unearth the records which lay in Buddhist monasteries waiting to be discovered; ola leaf records were collected and placed in the Governmental Oriental Library; later they were transferred to the Colombo Museum. Ancient ruins were brought back to life and light by jungle-exploring soldiers such as Lt Fagan who in 1820 wrote an account of his discoveries in the Ceylon Gazette. Subsequently, these records and inscriptions were studied by Sinhalese scholars and Civil Servants. The Ceylon Branch of the Royal Asiatic Society was founded in 1845 with the purpose of bringing to the notice of the Government the importance of salvaging the historical heritage of the island, its monuments and its records.

Thanks to the determination of Sir Arthur Gordon, an Archaeological Survey was then set up in 1890.[12] This is where young DAL began his career as a draughtsman.

In those days government service was the most coveted source of employment. It was steady, respectable and pensionable but the Archaeological Survey did not provide its local staff with pensions at the outset. Few Sinhalese entered the civil service or administrative service as their knowledge of the English was poor. It was not patriotism which had kept them away from learning English, rather it was circumstances. Missionary schools which thrived in the North were rare in the South except in the big cities. So the men from the North who spoke Tamil and English equally well, shared the few jobs available with the Burghers who descended from the white men.

105

The Muhandiram: Becoming a Spectre

The first photograph was given to me by another grand daughter of DAL whom I met by chance in Maryland some years ago. It depicts the man at the end of his life in Muhandiram costume. He must have been so proud of himself, I had thought to myself first. Later, I got the sense that this may have been the memory of a humiliation. It was a staging. Through this photograph he let himself be transformed from subject to object, he lost his humanity. Barthes wrote about this experience:

> the photograph ... represents that very subtle moment when ... I am neither subject nor object but a subject who feels he is becoming an object: I then experienced a microversion of death (of parenthesis). I am truly becoming a spectre.[13]

DAL served the Archaeological Department for his entire adult life. He joined as a young man in the capacity of Draughtsman and retired as Head Draughtsman in 1926 at the age of 57. In 1908 he and W.M. Fernando replaced a single more highly paid European assistant, Mr Still, while continuing as Draughtsmen assisted by two others.[14] As native gentlemen they were deemed qualified to carry on the work of Mr Still who was leaving the service of H.C.P. Bell, the head of the Archaeological Survey.[15] Upon retirement DAL was given the title of Muhandiram. Like many others before him and after, he accepted the honour, the bestowal of rank by a foreign colonial and illegitimate power. Did this make him a collaborator, did this give him what Peebles subtly called an 'appearance of majesty'?[16] The body can be assigned contrasting simultaneous meanings. The fact that he deemed it necessary to stand before a photographer for posterity confirms that DAL was not (to my regret) a rebel. But who was? Not any of the scions of the great families who had the means to resist resisted. DAL, unlike them, had also to earn a living.

So DAL dressed up in his Muhandiram costume and looked like what the British thought a noble Low-Country man should look like. He wore a long coat made of dark navy blue cloth with one row of gold loops and buttons. His collar was embroidered in gold and edged with a gold braid. His shoulder straps were edged with gold braid. His trousers were of the same material as the coat. He wore a pair of black shoes. He did not wear the helmet of black cloth which was part of the Muhandiram costume, nor did he carry the sword in his gold lace belt. Did he consider these too farcical?

DAL's life was very closely linked to that of H.C.P. Bell the first Archaeological Commissioner. Harry Charles Purvis Bell arrived in the island in 1873, having been appointed Writer in the Ceylon Civil Service. He remained there for the rest of his life, apart from three brief visits to the Maldive Islands and one cricketing tour in Madras. He found, wrote the two authors of his biography, 'not only a career but a raison d'etre in a culture of another people'.[17] He learned the local languages as well as the Maldivian language. In 1880 he was elected Honorary Secretary of the Royal Asiatic Society, Ceylon Branch and later became the Editor of the Society's journal.[18]

Among the governors of Ceylon, Sir Arthur Gordon had a very personal interest in archaeology. Wherever he went on tour he inspected ruins and took photographs. In the autumn of 1889 he determined that a regular Archaeological Survey should be established. It was when Bell was stationed at Kegalla that he came to be seconded to undertake the Archaeological Survey. Kegalla would be the first area of research and the Kegalla Report became a landmark in antiquarian studies in the island. In June 1890 Bell started work at Anuradhapura and the following ten years were possibly the happiest and most interesting of his life. In them he produced the seven detailed Progress Reports on Anuradhapura, the three Interim Reports on Sigiriya, and he commenced work at Polonnaruwa. In 1895 he was appointed as Archaeological Commissioner with a salary of Rs 9,600 and two years late his appointment was backdated to 1890.

The most dramatic of the episodes in Bell's career was the exploration of Sigiriya. By 1898 he had cleared most of the forest undergrowth overlaying the site of the ancient city and completed a topographical survey of the whole area. He had undertaken the thorough excavation from end to end of the citadel which stood on the summit of Sigiri Gala and of the two staircase approaches to the gallery along its western face. He had also secured facsimile copies in oils of virtually all of the paintings which had survived to that day in the rock pockets. Excavations were carried out in Anuradhapura, Mihintale and Polonnaruwa and in outlying sites such as Medirigiriya where a beautiful shrine stood on the highest point of the rock.[19]

The relationship between Bell and DAL was from Bell's accounts a very cordial one. DAL's writings are neutral on this matter. The only semblance of a personal testimony is his published account of his work at Medirigiriya. Reading between the lines one begins to see a human being with his prejudices and qualities. This is the only report where the man appears and where it is possible to get a sense of how DAL construed the world in which he lived and how he invested it with meaning.

Medirigiriya

In 1907 when the restoration of the Wata-da-ge at Polonnaruwa had been largely achieved, Bell sent DAL to clear the site at Medirigiriya, to take photographs and make drawings. DAL spent thee days there and his report was printed in the Annual Report for that year, preceded by a repeat of Bell's original account.[20]

Medirigiriya, lies six miles away from Divunankaḷadawula, the nearest village. Writing in 1897, Bell described it as an extensive rock outcrop, not very high, bifurcated by jungle in two stretches side by side. There are ample remains on one rock, a fair-sized Dagaba cave, pillared ruins and an inscribed pillar. Bell marvelled at the gem of Medirigiriya, its Wata-da-ge, a beautiful shrine which stands at the highest point of the rock.

DAL described his three-day expedition to Medirigiriya ten years later:

> *17 October 1907*. Started for Medirigiriya with half a dozen Moors and Sinhalese for axe and *katty* work and six other coolies (Tamils and Moors) with pickaxes, *mamoties* for excavating.

In this single sentence it is possible to appreciate the way in which DAL understood and perceived the society in which he lived and worked. He appeared to have absorbed unproblematically the racial categories of his colonial masters who had neatly compartmentalised groups along ethnic/racial lines. But for DAL, a man of a higher class who had mastered the written word, the language of his masters and had some education, there was little difference between the men who composed his labour force: Sinhalese, Tamil or Moors they were all 'coolies'. The use of the term 'coolie' by DAL was not surprising. By the early twentieth century, racial, religious and caste categories had entered administrative documents as norms. Pejorative terms were unabashedly used as in the draft of an ordinance ironically destined to 'provide for the well-being and control of immigrant labourers'. It was stated:

> In this ordinance, unless the context otherwise requires, coolie means any labourer or Kangany (commonly known as Indian coolie) or any Muhammedan (commonly known as Tulican).[21]

Just as these terms had become commonly used by the middle classes, ethnic, racial or religious qualifications were just as naturally used to qualify an individual. For DAL, his society was a fragmented one, where alongside Sinhalese there were clearly defined communities called Tamils and Moors.

After an unfortunate delay of five days due to the cart, which contained all necessary equipment—camera, cooking utensils and provisions—upsetting while going down the bank of the tank (*oya*), and having to be unloaded before being raised again, they reached Divulankadawala in the night. At the village, DAL inquired for the Arachchi but found out that he had gone away two days before with a sick child. The Vel Vidane was then contacted. He is described as 'a sickly person'. This characterisation denotes perhaps DAL's own concern and fear of sicknesses in the dry zone as well as a certain pride in being a healthy and strong man. The Vel Vidane explained that the village was a poor village 'where no provisions could be bought'. Rural poverty and food shortages were indeed common in the early twentieth century. After DAL explained that he needed no provisions but half a dozen men to show his party the way to Medirigiriya and to work for him as paid workers, the Vel Vidane was more cooperative and promised to send some men the next day. But to DAL's exasperation they were not there in the morning. The Vel Vidane, when contacted, once again promised they would be coming 'just now'. Finally DAL took the situation in hand and went to the village in search of the men, found them and promised to pay them at Medirigiriya itself. But 'one by one they disappeared and hid'. DAL gave no explanation why they refused to work except that the Vel Vidane had no influence on them. Many explanations could be suggested: the fear of the unknown; DAL was perceived as a modern man from the city whom they did not trust; the existence of caste tensions between the village headman and the Vel Vidane over the villagers he wished to select; lethargy due to malarial conditions or reluctance to hard work; local legends about Medirigiriya.

109

In the morning of 19 October, DAL inspected the Wata-da-ge. Some attempt had been made the year before at clearing land by villagers employed through the Revenue Officer. DAL first got the mess cleared and the undergrowth, which had been carelessly thrown burnt. By sunset the axemen had felled the trees inside the Wata-da-ge. The 'Sinhalese' then cleared the scrub on the portico of the Wata-da-ge.

On 20 October, the work was resumed. The 'Moor axemen' and Sinhalese felled, cut up and cleared away several small trees round the portico of the Wata-da-ge and to the north of it. DAL then proceeded to take three photographs and finish a sketch of the Wata-da-ge ground plan with all the measurements and rough drawings of two different kinds of pillars and their capitals. While the 'coolies' were having their evening meal, DAL and two men went exploring the site. Before they could go very far in the jungle, they came across the inscribed slab which had forty four lines of writing in Sinhalese. When it was dark, they made their way to the camp and found another slab oblong in shape, at the south side.

> 21 October: The 'axemen' and Sinhalese finished clearing the trees between the Wata-da-ge and the Dagaba on the north. Altogether twelve photographs were taken and six drawings made and measurements taken.

> 22 October: After taking their luggage and breakfast to Divulankadawala the cart was loaded and Hatmune was reached in the evening. On 23 October they reached Topanewa.

Nalanda Gedige, 1912

The Nalanda Gedige was, in the early twentieth century, a little known and solitary shrine of granite situated in the Central Province half-way between Matale and Dambulla. The Annual Report of 1910–11 gives a very detailed description of the shrine as it then appeared and of the surface ornaments and sculptures dug up around the temple. In 1912 DAL made drawings to scale of the temple as it then stood, and of the pillars and sculptured slabs so far unearthed, and supervised further digging.[22]

When Bell retired in 1911, the choice for his successor fell on Edward Russell Ayrton who had already had seven years' experience of excavation in Egypt. As it turned out his period of service was disastrously short. He drowned in 1914 in the tank near Tissamaharama and was buried nearby in the old Dutch Cemetery. A.M. Hocart took over in 1921.

Between 1914 and 1921 the work of the Archaeological Department was left in the charge of DAL under the nominal supervision of the North-Central Province Government Agent. These being colonial times, DAL was never made Archaeological Commissioner but awarded the title of Muhandiram on retirement.[23]

One gets a glimpse of the work DAL would have performed. In 1918 he provided an account of an inscribed pillar found within a quarter of a mile of the Abhayagiriya Dagaba. In his foreword to his article, Bell gave a general account of the development of scripts, from the archaic forms of the ninth and tenth centuries and as far as Mahinda IV, to those of the late twelfth and thirteenth centuries beginning under Parakramabahu I, and again to the types of the fourteenth and fifteenth centuries. DAL had sent Bell the text of the pillar, with transliteration, translation and an introduction, and both of them commented on the unusual inverted engraving, the lines running from right to left and from bottom to top of each side. This and other 'freak pillars' pointed to the reign of Sena II, here inscribed as Sri Sang Abaya, whom Bell dated from 866–891 A.D. though DAL following Wickremasinghe, preferred 917–952 A.D.. This *gal sannasa* bestowed a garden on monks of the Mangale Pirivena, near the Abhayagiriya Dagaba; and the location of the pillar confirmed its more recent identification.[24]

Although during the First World War, in the absence of a replacement for Ayrton, the Archaeological Commissioner who died tragically a few months after his arrival in Ceylon, DAL was put in charge of the Commission, few people remember him. He was the first native in charge of the Archaeological Department, the author of many joint articles published in the *Journal of the Royal Asiatic Society,* of most plans of ruined cities and monuments of the period 1900–20 and a stunningly talented artist. For all this work, at the end of his career he was bestowed the title of Muhandiram. So on that date, dressed up in this ornate costume, my great-grandfather, probably suffering from the intense heat and long period of posing for the photographer, looked into the camera, stood still for posterity and became a spectre.

Sigiriya and la Joie de vivre

The second photograph which appeared in *Twentieth-Century Impressions of Ceylon* represents DAL wearing a beret on his head, firmly standing in mid-air 150ft above ground, painting oil reproductions of the Sigiriya frescoes. He was the modern man, the creator, the artist. The photography conveys an impression of joy and freedom which none of the other photographs in the book even suggest.

112

Sigiriya always occupied a special place in the dreams of DAL. That rock which stood eleven miles from Polonnaruwa like a closed fist in the dry vegetation. He had painted her so many times. How could he not be part of her? That was where he suffered most and created his most beautiful and lasting work. The word Sigiriya is a compound of the two words 'Sinha' (lion) and 'giri' (rock). The legend of Sigiriya haunted him perhaps. Kassapa was the son of King Dhatusena (459–477 A.D.), who ruled in the capital of Anuradhapura, with a wife of unequal birth. Moggalana was the rightful heir born of the anointed queen. This was the beginning of the story of Sigiri-Gala. This granite rock was situated in the Matale district, some ten miles north-east of Dambulla and nearly twenty miles west of the ancient capital of Polonnaruwa. It rose like a giant molar to about six hundred feet, above seemingly endless paddy fields and artificial lakes. The nineteenth century was coming to an end when Sigiri-gala was rediscovered by British officers and administrators. For centuries the jungle and its beasts had taken over the rock, covered it with weeds and drowned it with whirs and drones unknown to human ears.

Kassapa ascended to the throne unable to kill Moggallana who escaped to India. After ordering the death of his father, Kassapa, fearing the inevitable return of Mogallana, decided to seek refuge in the 'inaccessible stronghold of Sihagiri'. At the summit of this rock, he built a magnificent palace which resembles Alakamanda—the abode of the god Kuvera. After Moggallana returned from India where he had gathered an army to fight Kassapa, the two brothers met on a battlefield. Kassapa, in order to avoid a stretch of marshy ground turned his elephant. His army misconstrued his move as sign of retreat and began to flee. The story goes that Kassapa slashed his own throat to avoid being captured. Moggalana had then handed over Sigiriya to the priesthood and established himself as King in Anuradhapura.

A later seventh-century record mentioned the execution of two kings in or near Sigiriya and a sixteenth-century book of Sinhalese verse entitled *Mandarampura* mentioned the villaged Sigiriya. After that no mention was made of the fortress. For long, Sigiriya remained unknown territory.

113

Major H. Forbes rode in search of the fortress in 1831 and again in 1833 and recorded his impressions of the walled gallery. Forbes never climbed beyond the base of the rock. But in 1853, two young civil servants reached the summit. Sigiriya was once again discovered and put on the map when Governor Gordon proposed to the Council to undertake a systematic examination of the ruins in Sigiriya before the monuments perished. He commissioned H.C.P. Bell to 'carry to completion the survey of either Sigiriya or Yapahuwa'. But it was not before 1895 that Sigiriya was actually thoroughly examined and became an archaeological site.[25]

The Frescoes

The frescoes were first sighted in 1875 by T.H. Blakesley of the Public Works Department who viewed them through field glasses as he was unable to make the perilous climb up to the fresco pocket. In 1889 Alick Amurray of the Public Works Department escalated the rock and slipped into the fresco pocket where he laboured for days to take tracings of thirteen of the figures. Later, like industrious ants, an army of workmen bored holes in the rock at regular intervals and side-iron jumpers were fixed in with cement, to which a wooden staging was secured. Within the pocket iron beams were carefully set in the rock surface and a working platform was arranged above the rotund floor of the pocket.

When DAL had first climbed Sigiriya the summit was unreachable even in his dreams. He had then ventured through the zig-zagging gallery quite confidently and climbed the slender bamboo ladder with the agility of an acrobat. He had then reached the cave containing the frescoes. The figures in the cave, all female, represented ladies of Kassapa's court, with their attendants carrying offerings of flowers to Piduragala, the *vihara* on the conical hill to the north of Sigiriya. Some of the ladies were yellow and orange, others greenish-blue. They wore ornaments, flowers and ribbons, their necks, breast and arms were loaded with jewels. They were nude from the waist upwards. Their bodies were cut off by clouds at the waist. He imagined them dancing around him, their unsupported breasts trembling delicately as they moved. When he saw them for the first time, after months of solitude, DAL had felt he was a conqueror receiving a royal greeting.

It is believed that there were five hundred depictions of women in this and other rock pockets although there were only twenty-one complete figures visible.

He had lain on his back on an improvised scaffolding for over nineteen weeks to get an adequate view of these ladies. He knew every curve of their bodies, every nuance of colour. He had a secret name for each one of them. Sometimes he sang to them hymns which he had learnt at school. During those weeks of suffering the morning heat had been unbearable, the sun kindling his face with a force that made him wince. Flies and other creatures had taken residence in the cave and had taken great pleasure in sitting on his paint brushes which were coloured with chrome yellow, burnt sienna, raw umber, Indian red, sap green, lamp black and flake white. There was no blue except when he looked up at the sky. But he did not do that too often, as after any jerky movement it took time for him to regain his equilibrium.

He had also produced 'an excellent oil painting to scale' of the two fresco pockets 'after a week's rocking into space'. The south-west monsoon and the winds had played with him, rocked and buffetted him but perhaps, admirers of beauty too, had let him live so that his drawings would sing the beauty of the *apsaras*. In DAL's work, Bell's yearning for a reproduction of the frescoes with a 'faithfulness almost perfect' was fulfilled in 1896–97. In the face of DAL's 'singular talent, unflagging patience and real courage' Murray's week-long adventure pales into insignificance. DAL's eyes were seriously affected by the long hours he spent in the intense gale beating upon the rock face. Bell himself mentions that DAL was 'sorely tried at times by inflammation of the eyes and attacks of fever'. After he finished his work he was ordered complete rest for six weeks.[26]

DAL's paintings were first displayed at a meeting of the Royal Asiatic Society. DAL was not present but Bell complemented his work:

> Not a line, not a flaw or abrasion, not a shade of colour, but has been patiently reproduced with the minutest accuracy.[27]

The *Third Report* by Bell was read at the Annual General Meeting held in the Colombo Public Hall. At this meeting on 22 December 1897, plans, drawings and photographs were exhibited as well as the whole set of facsimile copies in oils of the frescoes; and Bell himself read the paper. Over two hundred people were present. In his speech thanking the Governor for his attendance as patron, the Bishop of Colombo made a brief reference to DAL. In 1898 Bell was elected as an Honorary Member of the Society.[28]

DAL's twenty-two oil paintings hung for a while in the Colombo museum for all to see. DAL would never have foreseen that people would come from everywhere to see his drawings, and even pay money to climb up the rock. Today the paintings are no longer visible to the public.

Coolies, Draughtsman and Chiefs

My third photograph comes from the published book called *H.C.P. Bell. Archaeologist of Sri Lanka and the Maldives* where DAL is mentioned from time to time, an intermittent figure in the life of the great man. The photograph shows H.C.P. Bell and DAL with the workforce at Sigiriya. DAL seems the odd man out. He is neither coolie nor a Mahatheya (master). His dress, a black western style jacket worn over a white sarong, extols this status. He is what Michael Roberts would gracefully call a 'person in between'. Bell stands, with arms crossed, at the peak of the human pyramid, dominating DAL as well as the native workforce. The photo is annotated in his handwriting with one of his quotations from Scott's 'Lady of the Lake':

> Note the graceful pose of the Chief at the back
> These be Clan Alpine's warriors true,
> And Saxon, I am Roderick Dhu.

116   This photograph exemplifies to what extent the British vision of Ceylonese society was a vertically stratified one. The colour line separated the Europeans from the Burghers and the natives. Amongst the natives, education had produced an elite which cut across communal differences, but which occupied a position similar to but lower than that of the Burghers in British eyes, fitting unthreateningly into the social stratification based on race. Natives were believed to belong, above all to the Sinhalese, Tamil and Moor races. In the twentieth century colonial officials were openly disparaging of the people they ruled over. In 1906 the Colonial Secretary (Sir Alexander Ashmore) made the rather insensitive statement that Ceylonese were not employed in the higher posts of the public service because they were deficient in qualities of duty and honour. This led to a sizeable meeting of leading Ceylonese lawyers, doctors, merchants, clerks, law and medical students where the government was severely attacked, and the policy of recruitment to the public service 'as based on an unfounded assumption and on racial distinction' condemned.[29] The Archaeological Department was not devoid of similar prejudices although Bell's biographers do not emphasise him as a racialist.

It is in Bell's writings that DAL's life appears between the lines, as apropos. In 1890 Bell was allocated a staff of native assistant and clerk combined, a draughtsman and twenty coolies. By 1900 this had been increased by a second clerk, two extra draughtsmen and a European Assistant and a hundred men as a workforce. Bell describes the accommodation of his assistants as being worse off than the humblest overseer on a tea estate, being supplied only with a wattle and daub thatched hut. In a memorandum of 1902 the staff asked for an incremental system of pay and better accommodation.

Bell supported their demands.[30] Petitioning was the most common mode of protest for natives. In 1908 an average of 4,000 petitioners were received by the then Governor Sir Henry McCallum.[31]

The Memorandum which was addressed to the Lieutenant-Governor and Commander-in-Chief of the Island was handed to him personally by DAL and the head clerk. This document gives some meagre but invaluable details about the lifestyle of the men who staffed the Archaeological Survey. The head draughtsman's salary was 1,200 rupees per annum, the head clerk's 720 rupees, the same as the second draughtsman while the third and second clerk earned 540 rupees. All these men had served in the department for long periods, as in those days one rarely changed employment. DAL had worked in the Survey for twelve years, that is since 1890.

117

In a memorandum submitted by Bell in 1908 when re-organisation of the staffing was proposed, he suggested that instead of engaging a new European Assistant these two should be promoted to act jointly as his Assistants on a higher salary.

> Mr D.A.L. Perera, 1ˢᵗ draughtsman has served in the Archaeo-logical Survey Department for 18 years. Mr W.M. Fernando, 2ⁿᵈ draughtsman for 11 years. Mr Perera is admitted to be almost without equal in Ceylon as a draughtsman. His copies of the Sigiriya frescoes and architectural drawings of Polonnaruwa structures are sufficient testimony to his excep-tional talent ... To retain their services in the department—for both can easily command remunerative employment in Colombo—when saddled with double duties (as assistants and draughtsmen) the inducement of a small annual increment should be offered.[32]

Survey clerks and draughtsmen were subject to special disabilities. Not only were they not entitled to a pension, they were further debarred from subscribing to the Widows and Orphans Pension Fund. In addition they had to suffer the inevitable fever and the climate of the North Central province. But there is no evidence to show that their grievances were answered.

In the photograph, DAL appears dressed in a black jacket, most probably over a white sarong. He is bald. Bell wears the colonial cap or *sola topi*. This new form of hat was designed in the 1840s to protect imperial heads from the torturous rays of the tropical sun. It was made from the pith of the sola plant. It was light and bulbous. Its function soon got confused with its fabric and it became known to many as the sola topi. It was the distinctive nature of various forms of European headwear that inspired Indians to refer to Europeans as *topi wallas*.[33]

British obsession with dress related closely to their perception of the physical environment.

The combination of alien customs and climate induced a fear of the unknown and clothes provided an important means of physical as well as psychological protection.

The topis were supposed to protect them from the much feared sun while at the same time providing a distinctive type of headgear which made them immediately recognisable as Europeans.

Bell was in many ways a typical colonial administrator, but in others he was different. His attachment to the country he worked in was unusual. Bell never seems to have contemplated retiring to England, but was happy to make his permanent home in the island. His biography describes him as self-centered, irrascible, meticulous, opinionated but with a strong appreciation of good work and a love of beauty in both nature and art. Although Bell worked without technical support at a time when scientific methods of excavation and conservation were in their infancy, his archaeological survey plans are still of immense service. Paranavitana described him as the pioneer of Ceylonese archaeology.

The 'Coolies'

The workforce of children, women and men sit at the feet of the pyramid. The women and children who are fewer in number crouch in front displaying their burned faces and worn out clothes. Most women are wearing coloured sarees tied over one shoulder. Except for one of them none of the others is wearing a blouse. Their heads are bare exposing their black hair tied behind their heads in a bun. The children are dressed in white sarongs and keep their heads covered with a turban.

The photograph tells us of their determination to survive the harsh conditions in which they were employed. But of their own lives and of their relationship with their superiors we can only venture a few hypotheses. The turbans worn by the menfolk can lead us to believe that they are Tamil workers. We know that Tamil workers from Anuradhapura were employed by the Archaeological Survey for the actual excavation. Local Sinhalese labour was employed in the extensive clearing of the whole area of the ancient city. In Sigiriya in 1896, some Sinhalese were used as earth carriers upon the top of the rock in consideration of the higher rate of wage paid for jungle-clearing below. Sinhalese workers were before that scared to scale the rock due to fear of demons. But generally the workforce hailed either from South India or were Tamils from adjoining areas. South Indians were very frequently employed in the public service departments such as the railways or the harbour. They were considered hard workers and more docile than the Sinhalese. It was common as in the Harbour strike of 1901 that South Indian labour was brought in to replace the strikers obviously at an inferior wage.[34] South Indian labour seldom protested against conditions of labour. In Sigiriya, Bell reported that there had been no accidents nor any deaths from disease, although there were cases of dysentery and fever and ulcerated sores caused by bad water. In 1897 he wrote:

119

> The climate of Sigiriya has usually proved bracing to the coolies, the majority of whom live for two-thirds of the year in the jungle *bund chenas* and low-lying lands about Anuradhapura. Month by month they 'put on flesh' despite the unspeakable heat which an eight hours spell of work upon the bare rocks involves: and return after the four months absence, robust and sleek, with a stock of health that enables them to battle better against the insidious malaria of the North Central Province.[35]

It appears then that the workforce was composed of *chena* cultivators from the Anuradhapura lowlands who work seasonally as cultivators and when required, perform hard work for the Archaeological Survey. Their working conditions were harsh: coolies worked continuously from 6.30 in the morning to 3.00 in the afternoon. They were not permitted to descend the rock for a mid-day meal. 'It would have entailed undue waste of time and energy' according to Bell.

This photograph exemplifies the less glorious nature of colonial archaeological work and the dilemma of DAL who belonged to a small group of people who had no option but to comply.

120

A Need for Memories

This chapter is about the writing of a history which interlinks biography and social history and in so doing surmises my own engagement in this enterprise in a reflexive manner. Writing these very words make me think about the discipline, to which I have devoted so much time. The task of the historian is to transform into history this need for memories. Simply recording events makes no sense. One must understand why and how things happened. This paper is also about me. Why at this particular moment of my life I try to understand a particular historical object says something of my own dreams and haunts and feeds into those of the man whose life and society I try to relieve and recreate.

Between the historian and his object is a friendship that must originate, if the historian wants to understand, for according to St Augustinus' formula 'one cannot understand anyone unless through friendship'. The man to whom I extend a hand of friendship is my own great-grandfather whom neither I nor my mother ever met. But although he died before she was born, she knows him. Each family has a great ancestor, a mythic figure about whom stories are told. DAL is perhaps my own thread to the colonial past which I can only imagine through otherwise neutral sources. He is my emotional terrain, my subjective other; he is perhaps what I might have been, had I been born as a man in another age. This paper is in many ways, a homage to this man who in the very limited space that was made available to him, chose to express his freedom by excelling in his work.

NOTES

1. Cited in Diana Fuss. 'Fashion and the Homospectatorial Look' in Kwame Anthony Appiah and Henry Louis Gates Jr. (eds.). *Identities*. Chicago: Chicago University Press, 1995: 105.

2. *Sarasavi Sanderesa*, 21 July 1889: 1.

3. *Sri Lankagana*. 1 March 1924: 2.

4. *Plate Ceylone Annual*, 1932.

5. Jacques Le Goff. *Histoire el Memoire*. Paris, Gallimard: 161–62.

6. Alain Corbin. *Le Village des Cannibales*. Paris: Aubier. 1990; Pierre Duby. *Le Dimanche de Bouvines, 27 Juillet 1214*. Paris: Gallimard. 1973.

7. Pierre Nora cited in Antoin Prost. *Douze Leçons sur L'Histoire*. Paris: Seuil. 1996: 300.

8. *The Examiner*. 4 August 1869.

9. *The Lakrivikirana*. Almanac, 8 January 1869.

10. *Ceylon Handbook and Directory* 1903–1904. Colombo, A.M.J. Ferguson. 1904: 41.

11. *Twentieth-Century Impressions of Ceylon*. 114.

12. B.N. and H.M. Bell. *H.C.P. Bell. Archaeologist of Ceylon and the Maldives*. London: Archetype Publ. 1993: 26–41.

13. Cited in Diana Fuss: 106.

14. *Administrative Report*, 1908.

15. Bell & Bell, *Op.cit.*: 125.

16. P. Peebles. *Social Changes in Nineteenth-Century Sri Lanka*. Delhi: Navrang. 1995.

17. B.N.Bell and H.M.Bell. *H.C.P.Bell: Archaeologist of Ceylon and the Maldives*. Denbigh, Archetype. 1993.

18. Bell & Bell. *Op.cit.*: 13.

19. Bell & Bell. *Op.cit.*: see especially Chapters 7 and 16–17.

20. *Archaeological Survey of Ceylon, Annual Report*, 1907: 30–32.

21. SLNA, 5/326, enclosed in despatch from Governor to Secretary of State, 17 March 1920.

22. *Archaeological Survey of Ceylon, Annual Report*, 1910–1911.

23. Bell & Bell. *Op.cit.*: 201.

24. Ceylon Antiquary and Literary Register, Vol. 4/2. 1918, 102–108.

25. Bell & Bell. *Op.cit.*: 63–101.

26. Archaeological Survey of Ceylon, Third Interim Report, 1897.

27. Interim Report, 1896: 258.

28. Bell & Bell. *Op.cit.*: 101.

29. V.K. Jayawardena. *The Rise of the Labour Movement in Ceylon.* Colombo, Sanjiva Prakasaya, 1972: 130.
30. ELNA 6/13432 B, ELNA 6/13255D.
31. V.R. Jayawardena. *Op.cit.*: 20.
32. Bell & Bell. *Op.cit.*: 51–52.
33. Emma Tarlo. *Clothing Matters*: 32.
34. V.R. Jayawardena. *Op.cit.*: 108.
35. *Interim Report Royal Asiatic Society*, 1897.

Chapter Six

CONCLUSION

Dress is one way of understanding the nature of late colonialism, and the permutations and changes in social and power relations that shook the last decades of British rule. Indeed each society, each civilisation each period of time works on the body of its members to sculpt them in its image, according to its values and for its own ends. The essays in this book grapple with the ways in which dress, as it covers the human body, gives meaning and value, sends messages of love and pain, liberates and oppresses at one and the same time.

This volume has demonstrated that dress was above all an object of consumption that evolved with Sri Lanka's encounter with colonialism. The evolution of patterns of dress consumption and production can only be understood within the broader picture of a small state being gradually integrated into the network of world capitalism. The sewing machine was the epitome of modernity and with its large-scale adoption the nature of people's relation to clothes and dress-making changed dramatically.

Dress was also a potent identity-marker. Early nationalists invented a staid national dress for men—a white sarong and shirt with a draped shawl—and declared the Kandyan or Up-Country saree—the osariya—to be the most adequate dress for women. The cloth and jacket with its various Dutch-style collars, frills, cuffs and hemlines worn by women on the southern coast was considered too hybrid to be suitable. The osariya was conceived to be not only a moral dress but also the authentic Sinhala costume by the Sinhala literati of the early twentieth century—the reason being that the Kandyan kingdom had been the last to fall to colonial powers.

Just as the nature of nationalism or rather nationalisms can be understood through positions taken vis-a-vis the national dress, the violence of colonialism seeped out of the decrees that pertained to uniforms and official dress and the invention of traditions such as the 'traditional Kandyan shoe' practised by colonial rulers.

Of course even a subject people did not accept all the codes of conduct laid down for them. The relation to the body was far from being natural and immediate and took them into a labyrinth of reflections: each person had first to lose himself/herself if s/he wanted to transcend the illusion of a non-existent body and construct through this language a dual body for himself/herself and the other in which s/he tried to recognise himself/herself. Some people chose to dress as the British did—D.S. Senanayake was one of them—others wore a hybrid outfit—a western coat and sarong like the draughtsman of the previous chapter. The majority, for whom dress was not a conscious object of thought, continued wearing the outfits they found most convenient. The evolution of dress in Sri Lanka can thus be read as a series of 'strategies of distinction' by social groups, communities and individuals stepping in and out of various types of outfits and often, in so doing, taking positions. Dress under colonial rule was politics without the risks involved.

The politics of dress has remained with us into the twenty-first century. In many ways the issues involved stem from the colonial period referred to in this book. As travel outside the island is ever more common, identity is often projected for the other through dress: Sri Lankan women living or working in the West are for instance recognised as those wearing frilly sarees—the osariya—an attire distinct and different from that of Indian women. In Sri Lanka itself, in some sectors the saree remains the 'national dress' but with distinctions within. For instance, whether worn in the Kandyan or Indian style it still reigns supreme both as the dress of the professional woman—who tends to prefer cotton and silk sarees from India—and as the dress for all rites of passage. But its cost and the care needed—starching and ironing—has recently led to the general adoption of synthetic sarees by the less affluent classes of saree-wearers. Initially a democratic dress, the saree is now the site of subtle stratifications.

125

Unlike in India, where the shalwar-kameez became the popular sartorial compromise of east-west or different cultures, in Sri Lanka it remains a marginal/uncommon form of dress. In rural areas it is still perceived as the dress of the Muslim community while in the city it is seldom worn by professional women. There is indeed a certain perception of shalwar-kameez wearers: Teledramas, for instance, would portray a social worker as bespectacled, wearing a shalwar-kameez and carrying a large bag. It is a fact that as a work outfit the shalwar-kameez is endorsed by the non-governmental sector, actors and young academics. As leisure wear it has also been adopted by many young women who seek to look modern without appearing western and to look South Asian without appearing traditional. In a sense for women in Sri Lanka, the shalwar-kameez is a South Asian identity marker rather than, as in India, a nationally integrative dress.

The most important sartorial change of the last two decades has come with the liberalisation of the economy and the growth of an export-oriented garment industry. This has made available in the marketplace an entire range of western-type brand name clothes, jeans, T-shirts, skirts sold at a very reasonable price. The less affluent classes, concerned rather with practical problems of price and availability than with fashion, have enthusiastically shed their cloth and jacket, synthetic saree and sarong for more globalised outfits.

If jeans are commonly wore by young men of all social classes in Sri Lanka, there are significant gender difference: jeans remain confined to a minute highly westernised female population. The notion of shame—*lajja*—is crucial to explain the reluctance on the part of young women to adopt jeans or to wear skirts above their knees. Jeans that hug the body are considered to be too revealing. Unlike Islam, Buddhism is not specific about modesty in men and women although among radical Sinhalese nationalists it is frequent to hold a very moralistic discourse on clothes. Dress codes remain, for most women part of a patriarchal and authoritarian system which allows for little deviance.

126

Dress, in a multi-ethnic society, is one of the most powerful means of showing belonging or distance from the majority group or the mainstream. Jaffna Tamils today dress just as they did during the colonial period. However, distance from the Sinhalese majority is stressed in other ways through the adoption of particular turbans or caps. Coast Moors and Malays tend to tie a handkerchief on their head differentiating themselves from Ceylon-born Moors who wear a fez which is often red in colour. In a country with a variegated population, national dress can only be that of one single group of the population, generally the majority group, and is therefore usually a social construction. The national dress that was eventually adopted in Sri Lanka was a clever exercise in compromise. From the 1950s, politicians and statesmen as different as J.R. Jayawardena and R. Premadasa wore the national dress in public. The first did so perhaps to hide his upper-class identity, the second to display his working class credentials. Others have adopted a hybrid version of the national dress, for example dropping the sarong for a pair of white trousers. The present Prime Minister, Ranil Wickremasinghe, who tries to project the image of a man of the future, is never seen in full national dress. Members of the newly reconstituted JVP stand out by consciously refusing to wear anything even faintly resembling ethnic wear. Their concession to fashion is limited to wearing red shirts and plain trousers. The present JVP leader, following the trend set by Che Guevara and emulated by Rohana Wijeweere, wears a beret. In this sense their radicalism is expressed sartorially in a denial of tradition and an empathy with the working class of the world rather than with the poorer classes of their own country.

Guerillas and former guerrillas have understood the power of dress. Their usage of dress varies from army-type uniforms to minimal symbols such as slouch hats, coloured armbands and ties. With its history of ethnic and civil violence, Sri Lanka is a laboratory for research on guerrilla dress. The main Tamil militant group, the LTTE, has discarded civilian dress and wears conventional uniforms, thus portraying itself as a government in exile representing an organised and modern state of Eelam. Dress legitimates this claim. In this way the LTTE resembles IRA members who proclaim their identity sartorially at funerals. The JVP in its two incarnations in 1971 and in the late 1980s used another tactic of modern guerrilla warfare which was to erase boundaries between the group and civilians, thus gaining the advantage of concealment. The survival of guerrillas and of governments depends to a large extent on their ability to communicate through symbolic means, and dress is a crucial component in the image they wish to project.

127

Men's national dress never really caught on in Sri Lanka either as office wear or as casual wear, perhaps simply because it was not elegant enough. While a variation of the osariya is worn by the stewardesses on the Sri Lanka national airline, the stewards typically wear a wine-coloured jacket over a pair of trousers similar to the costume of a Parisian waiter. In Sri Lanka quite clearly, the man is not expected to represent and embody the nation and its pride. The national dress is today more costume than dress, worn only by politicians and public figures and sometimes as a wedding outfit. Its failure can be traced to the lower-class connotation of the sarong at a time when the younger generation, yearning for social mobility and modernity, can so easily turn the tables and become *Mahatthayas* (Sirs) by adopting trousers. The sarong may very well disappear in the rural areas except as night wear and we may no longer see men bent in two with their sarongs folded over their heads during the monsoon rains!

The sarong has, however, been given a new lease of life with the growth of what can be termed ethnic chic: the upper classes' predilection for sarongs made of expensive silk or handloom as evening wear. In the face of the levelling influence of the western trousers there is the peculiar desire of the privileged to distinguish themselves, whatever the cost, from the masses who follow them, to set up a barrier. The upper classes have constantly to invent new 'gilded costumes'. Recently, a former star batsman had a party where guests— both men and women—were invited to come dressed in sarongs. Many designers—Barbara Sansoni is the most successful—and garment producers have realised the potential of ethnic chic in Sri Lanka. Handlooms and raw cotton have been given a new lease of life, thanks to the elite's desire to return to its roots. The paradox is that elites are stepping into village dress at the very moment that the majority of people are stepping out of it. The changes taking place are not dissimilar to a carnival where the tables have been turned and master and slave have enthusiastically traded dress and body.

APPENDIX

Uniform For Muslims

Rank.	Coat.	Sarong.	Sash.	Headwear.	Footwear.	Sword.	Sword Belt.
Gate Mudaliyars	Long coat of white silk or white broad cloth with gold loops and buttons	Sarong with white as predominant colour	Colour optional	Turkish turban with white as predominant colour	If footwear is used, jutas without socks or shoes (black or white) with socks or stockings to match. Jutas must be removed in the presence of the Governor	Hilt gold and scabbard of silver inlaid with gold.	Spangled gold lace to be worn over the right shoulder or girded round the loins
Mudaliyars ..	do. ..	do.	do. ..	do.	do. ..	Silver inlaid with gold	do. ..
Muhandirams ..	do.	do.	do. ..	do. ..	do. ..	Hilt and scabbard of silver, hilt only inlaid with gold	Plain gold lace, not spangled, to be worn over the right shoulder or girded round the loins

Uniform For Kandyan Sinhalese

Rank.	Jacket.	Tippet.	Shirt.	Trousers.	Belt.	Sword and Sword Belt.	Footwear.	Headwear.	Other Items of Uniform.
Adikar. (i) State dress	.. Gold embroidered jacket, or *pesa bettaya* the sleeves coming to the elbow or long sleeves	*Mante* or tippet of white muslin edged with gold lace	*Reli Kamise*, or shirt with frills (not to be European dress shirt)	*Sudu Reli Kalisam* or frilled trousers	Of gold lace or spangled with gold	Silver hilted sword (not *kastane*), sheath red velvet mounted in silver. Sword belt of red velvet with a narrow edge of gold lace.	The wearing of jutas, which are the only footwear allowed to be worn is optional. If jutas are worn, white socks must	Four-cornered hat in red or green with *deti* and *Malgaha*	1. *Kasau tuppotti* 2. Dagger 3. Necklaces and rings 4. *Pata tahaduwa* or gold fillet 4¾ inches long and 1¹/₃ deep in the middle fastened by silk strings

Continues...

Contd...

Rank.	Jacket.	Tippet.	Shirt.	Trousers.	Belt.	Sword and Sword Belt.	Headwear.	Footwear.	Other Items of Uniform.
						Sword should hang straight at the side, the belt passing over the right shoulder		also be worn	5. Staff, silver, curved at the top slightly ornamented with gold
(ii) Semi-State dress	.. Instead of the gold embroidered jacket, a white jacket of the same shape should be worn. (In Uva this jacket may have long sleeves)	do. ..	do. ..	do. ..	do. ..	Sword will not be worn	do. ..	do. ..	1. *Kasaa tuppotti* 2. Dagger 3. Staff, silver, curved at the top, slightly ornamental with gold The wearing of necklaces and rings is optional
(iii) Undress (for attendance at the Kachcheries and Courts and at minor public functions)	do...	Wearing of *mante* optional	do. ..	do. ..	No belt.	do. ..	White square hat with *Malgaba* or *borale*	do. ..	1. Ordinary *sudu tuppotti* 2. Staff, silver, curved at the top, slightly ornamented with gold The wearing of necklaces and rings is optional

The Adikar has the privilege on State Occasions of having whips cracked before him throughout the Kandyan Provinces.

Disawa.

Rank.	Jacket.	Tippet.	Shirt.	Trousers.	Belt.	Sword and Sword Belt.	Headwear.	Footwear.	Other Items of Uniform.
(i) State dress	.. Gold embroidered jacket or	*Mante* or tippet of white muslin	*Reli Kamise* or shirt with	*Sudu Reli Kalisam*	Of gold lace, or spangled	No sword	..Four-cornered hat in red	The wearing of jutas, which are	1. *Kasaa tuppotti* 2. Dagger 3. Necklaces and rings

Continues...

131

Contd...

Rank.	Jacket.	Tippet.	Shirt.	Trousers.	Belt.	Sword and Sword Belt.	Headwear.	Footwear.	Other Items of Uniform.
	pesabettaya the sleeves coming to the elbow	edged with gold lace	frills (not to be European dress shirt)	or frilled trousers	with gold	No sword	with *deti* and *Malgaha*	the only footwear allowed to be worn, is optional. If jutas are worn, white socks must also be worn	4. *Pata tabaduwa* or gold fillet $4^{3/4}$ inches long and $1^{1/3}$ deep in the middle fastened by silk strings
(ii) Semi-dress	..Instead of the gold embroidered jacket, a white jacket of the same shape should be worn. (In Uva this jacket may have long sleeves)	*Mante* or tippet of white muslin edged with gold lace.	*Reli Kamise* or shirt with frills (not to be European dress shirt)	*Sudu Reli Kalisam* or frilled trousers	Of gold lace or spangled with gold	No sword	..Four-cornered hat in red with *deti* and *malgaha*	The wearing of jutas, which are the only footwear allowed to be worn, is optional. If jutas are worn, white socks must also be worn	1. *Kasau tuppotti* 2. Dagger The wearing of necklaces and rings is optional
(iii) Undress (for attendance at the Kachcheries and Courts and at minor public functions)	do. ..	..Wearing of *mante* optional	do. ..	do. ..	No belt..	do. ..	..White square hat with *malgaha* or *borale*	do. ..	1. Ordinary *sudu tuppotti* The wearing of necklaces and rings is optional

Continues...

Contd...

Rank.	Jacket.	Tippet.	Shirt.	Trousers.	Belt.	Sword and Sword Belt.	Headwear.	Footwear.	Other Items of Uniform.
A Disawa has the privilege on State Occasions of having tom-toms beaten him in his Disawani.									
Rate or Disawe or Atapattuwe Lekam, Rate Adikaram, Disawe Mohottale, Atapattuwa Mohottale.									
(i) When the Adikar or Disawa appears in full dress	A white jacket the sleeves coming to the elbow. (In Uva this jacket may have long sleeves)	Wearing of *mante* optional	*Reli Kamise* or shirt with frills (not to be European dress shirt)	No trousers	No belt	No sword	White round hat ..	do. ..	1. Ordinary *sudu tuppotti*
(ii) When the Adikar or Disawa appears in undress	do. ..	do. ..	do. ..	do. ..	do. ..	do. ..	Round hat coloured with gold work or white—with out *deti*	do. ..	do. ..
Ratemahatmayas, Chief Interpreters and Interpreters of Kandyan birth, of Kachcheries, and Presidents, Village Tribunals, Muhandiram Nilame and Kankanam Nilame of the Attapattu Murapolu.									
(i) State Dress	Gold embroidered jacket or *pesabettaya* the sleeves coming to the elbow	*Mante* or tippet of white muslin edged with gold lace. (Presidents to wear without gold border)	do. ..	*Sudu Reli Kalisam* or frilled trousers	Of gold lace or spangled with gold	Nil	Four-cornered hat in red with *deti* or *malgaha*	do. ..	1. *Kasau tuppotti* 2. Dagger 3. Necklace and rings

Continues...

Contd...

Rank.	Jacket.	Tippet.	Shirt.	Trousers.	Belt.	Sword and Sword Belt.	Headwear.	Footwear.	Other Items of Uniform.
(ii) Semi-dress	.. Instead of the gold embroidered jacket, a white jacket of the same shape should be worn. (In Uva this jacket may have long sleeves)	do. ..	do. ..	do. ..	do. ..	Nil	do. ..	do. ..	1. *Kasau tuppotti* 2. Dagger The wearing of necklaces and rings is optional
(iii) Undress (for attendance at the Kachcheries and Courts and at minor public functions)	do. ..	Wearing of *mante* optional	do. ..	do. ..	Nil	Nil	White square hat with *malgaha* or *borale*	do. ..	1. Ordinary *sudu tuppotti* The wearing of necklaces and rings is optional

Temple Chiefs.
Diyawadane Nilame
Basnayake Nilames
  (i) State dress ⎤
  (ii) Semi-dress ⎬ Same as that prescribed for Ratemahatmayas.
  (iii) Undress ⎦

Source: Ceylon Government Gazette, Part I (General), 17 April 1935: 577.

GLOSSARY

Adigar	Chief officer of state in the Kandyan kingdom
Almairah	Cupboard
Arachchi	Traditional official
Arya	High status obtainable through the performance of meritorious acts
Batgam	Sinhalese caste associated with palanquin bearing and guard duty
Bhikku	An ordained Buddhist monk
Bund chena	Chena land along the bund of a tank
Chakra	Lit.wheel, circle; denotes the 'wheel of becoming' or 'round of existence'; also the spinning wheel
Chena	Forest land brought under cultivation by the slash and burn method

Comboy	Type of cloth originally imported from Cambay, Gujarat
Coolie	1. Kuli, aboriginal tribe of Gujarat 2. generally unskilled labour
Dagaba	Edifice built over a relic; generally a dome-shaped monument
Dalada maligawa	Temple of the Sacred Tooth in Kandy
Day Perahera	Ritual or religious procession held during the day
Gal sannasa	Royal grant inscribed in stone
Gedige	Building encompassing a shrine
Goyigama	Sinhalese caste, cultivators
Jataka	Tales relating the previous births of Gautama Buddha
Kangani	Recruitment agent for immigrant plantation labour; labour supervisor on the estate
Karawa	Sinhalese caste; fishermen
Katty	English for Kaththa; an instrument for hacking things
Korale	An administrative unit of a province or Disavani
Low-Country	Districts in the western and southern provinces, the Chilaw district or the western part of the Puttalam
Mahavamsa	Lit. 'Great Chronicle': Book composed in four parts, the first in the sixth century, the second in the thirteenth, the third in the fourteenth and the last in the eighteenth. In the European edition only the first part is called the *Mahavamsa*. The latter parts form the *Culavamsa*.
Mamoty	large spade
Mudaliyar	A chief headman; until the eighteenth century, a civil and military officer; an administrator of a korale in British times; Also used, only in the Low-Country, as an honorary title from the mid-nineteenth century.
Muhandiram	1. Assistant to a Mudaliyar; 2. An honorary title
Nikaya	Buddhist sect
Nilame	High official; chief

Pirith	Ritual chanting of Buddhist texts
Poya day	Full moon day
Rajakariya	Service. In the Kandyan kingdom, this encompassed service to the King, a lord, or the temple. In British times, it denoted compulsory service to the state, as well as to a lord or the temple
Tombo	List or register of people/lands
Sangha	Order of Buddhist monks
Sarong	Body cloth stitched together at both ends, commonly worn by Sinhalese men
Up-Country	Districts in the central and north-central provinces—the provinces of Uva and Sabaragamuwa, the Kurunegala district and part of the Puttalam district, the Sinhalese divisions of the districts of Batticaloa, Trincomalee and Millaitivu
Veddah	Last descendants of the ancient inhabitants of Sri Lanka, pre-dating the official arrival of the Sinhalese
Vel Vidana	Village level official in charge of paddy fields
Vidana Arachchi	Village-level official

BIBLIOGRAPHY

Primary Sources

Unpublished Sources

Public Records Office, Kew
Colonial Office Records
co 54 series
co 59 series
co 537 series

Rhodes House Library, Oxford

Papers of Sir Matthew Nathan: papers relating to the Special
Commission on the Constitution (Donoughmore) oral and written

evidence given by witnesses before the Commission and miscellaneous papers relating to Ceylon, 1929–1932.

Sri Lanka National Archives

Lots 4 and 5   Despatches to Secretary of State 1920 to 1947

Printed Sources

Primary sources

139

Government Publications

Archaeological Survey of Ceylon, Third Interim Report, 1897.

Archaeological Survey of Ceylon, Annual Report, 1907.

Archaeological Survey of Ceylon, Annual Report, 1910–1911.

Ceylon Antiquary and Literacy Register, Vol. 4/2 1918.

Ceylon, *Return of the Population of the Maritime Districts of the Island of Ceylon*, Colombo, 1816.

Ceylon, *Census of Ceylon*, 1824.

Ceylon, *Census of the Island of Ceylon 1871, General Report*, Registrar General's Office, Colombo, 1873.

Ceylon, *Census of the Island of Ceylon 1881 General Report and Statements and Tables*, Colombo, 1882.

Ceylon, *Census of the Island of Ceylon* 1901, Vol.1, H.C. Cottle, Acting Government Printer, Ceylon, 1902.

Ceylon, *Ceylon Administrative Report* 1895.

Ceylon, *Ceylon Administrative Report of the Government Agent of the Southern Province*, 1905, H.C. Cottle Government Printer Ceylon, 1906.

Ceylon Administrative Report 1908, Colombo.

Ceylon Government Gazette, April 17, 1935, No. 8.116.

Ceylon Almanach and Compendium of Useful Information 1821.

Denham, E.B., *Ceylon At the Census of 1911*, H.C. Cottle, Government Printer Ceylon, 1912.

Command Papers 3131, Ceylon Report of the Special Commission on the Constitution of Ceylon, July 1928.

English and vernacular Newspapers (selected years)

Arya Sinhala Wansaya, 1913, 1918.

Dinamina, 1931.

Lakmina, 1895.

Lankadipa, 1948.

Nidahasa, 1948.

Sarasavi Sanderesa Saha Sinhala Samaja, 1924.

Sarasavi Sanderesa, 1889.

Sri Lankangana, 1924.

The *Ceylon Daily News*, 1931, 1948, 1956.

The *Ceylon Examiner*, 1896.

The *Ceylon Independent*, 1903, 1904.

The *Ceylon Observer*, 1897, 1948.

The *Examiner*, 1869.

The *Lakvirikirina Almanak*, 1869.

The *London Times*, 1960.

The *Sinhala Jatiya*, 1913, 1921, 1923.

The *Times of Ceylon*, 1948.

The *Times of London*, 1957, 1963.

Young Ceylon, 1932.

Books

A'malvi, Christian, 1997. 'Le 14 Juillet. Du Dies Irae a Jour de Fete'. In Pierre Nora, (ed.) *Les Lieux de Memoire*, Paris, Gallimard. pp.439–460

Amin, Shahid. 1995. *Event, Metaphor, Memory. Chauri Chaura 1922–1992*. New Delhi, Oxford University Press.

Anderson, B. 1991. *Imagined Communities. Reflections on the Origin and Spread of Nationalism*. Revised and extended 2ⁿᵈ ed. London & New York, Verso.

————.1998, *The Spectre of Comparisons. Nationalism. Southeast Asia and the World*. London, Verso.

Appadurai, A. (ed.) 1986. *The Social Life of Things: Commodities in Cultural Perspective*. New York, Cambridge University Press.

Barnes, R. and J. Eicher (eds.) 1992. *Dress and Gender: Making and Meaning*. Providence, R.I. Berg.

141

Barthes, Roland. 1957. *Mythologies*. Paris, Edition du Seuil.

Bell, Bethia N. and Heather M. Bell. 1993. *H.C.P. Bell, Archaeologist of Ceylon and the Maldives*. Denbigh, Archetype Publications.

Bourdieu, P. 1984. *Distinction: A Social Critique of the Judgement of Taste*. London, Routledge and Kegan Paul.

Braudel, F. 1984. *Civilisation and Capitalism, Fifteenth to Eighteenth Century, Vol.1: The Structure of Everyday Life*. London, William Collins Sons & Co. Ltd.

————.1988. *The Identity of France*, Vol.1, New York, Harper and Row.

Burke, T. 1996. 'Sunlight Soap has Changed my Life: Hygiene, Commodification and the Body in Colonial Zimbabwe'. In H. Hendrickson (ed.) *Clothing and Difference. Embodied Identities in Colonial and Post-Colonial Africa*. Durham and London, Duke University Press: pp 189–212.

Callaway, Helen.1993. 'Dressing for Dinner in the Bush. Rituals of Self-Definition and British Imperial Authority'. In R. Barnes and J. Eicher (eds.) *Dress and Gender: Making and Meaning*, Providence, RI/Oxford Berg.

Chaudhuri, N.C. 1976. *Culture in the Vanity Bag*. Jaico, Bombay.

Comaroff, J.L. and J. Comaroff 1992. 'Bodily Reform as Historical Practice'. In, J.L. Comaroff and J. Comaroff (eds). *Ethnography and the Historical Imagination*. Boulder, Westview: pp. 69–81.

Corbin, Alain. 1990. *Le Village des Cannibales*, Paris, Aubier.

Cordiner, J. 1983. *Description of Ceylon Containing an Account of the Country, Inhabitants and Natural Productions 1807*, Vol.1, Dehiwala, Tisara Prakasakayo.

Cordwell, M. and R.A. Schwartz (eds.) 1979. *The Fabrics of Culture: The Anthropology of Clothing and Adornment*. The Hague, Mouton.

Cohn, B. 1983. 'Representing Authority in Victorian India'. In E. Hobsbawn and T. Ranger (eds.). *The Invention of Tradition*, Cambridge, Cambridge University Press: pp.165–210.

————.1990. 'The Census, Social Structure and Objectification in South Asia'. In *An Anthropologist Among the Historians and Other Essays*. Delhi, Oxford University Press: pp.224–354.

Darnton, Robert. 1985. *The Great Cat Massacre and Other Episodes in French Cultural History*. New York, Vintage Books.

De Alwis, Malathi. 1997. 'The Production and Embodiment of Respectability: Gendered Demeanours in Colonial Ceylon'. In Michael Roberts (ed.) *Sri Lanka. Collective Identities Revisited*, Vol.1, Colombo, Marga Institute: pp.105–143.

de Beauvoir, S. 1949. *Le Deuxieme Sexe*, Vol.1, Paris, Gallimard.

Ceylon Handbook and Directory 1903–04. 1904. Colombo, A.M.J. Ferguson.

De Croisset, F. 1926. *La Feerie Cinghalaise. Ceylon avec les Anglais*, Paris, J. Ferenczi et fils.

Dharmadasa, K.N.O. 1992. *The Growth of Sinhalese Nationalism in Sri Lanka*, Michigan, Michigan Press.

————.1997. 'The Sinhala Buddhist Identity and the Nayakkar Dynasty in the Politics of the Kandyan Kingdom, 1739–1815'. In M. Roberts (ed.) *Sri Lanka. Collective Identities Revisited*, Vol.1, Colombo, Marga Institute: pp.79–104.

Duby, Pierre. 1973. *Le Dimanche de Bouvines*, 27 Juillet 1214. Paris, Gallimard.

Ehrenfeis, U.R. von. 1979. *The Fabrics of Culture. The Anthropology of Clothing and Adornment*. The Hague, Mouton.

Ferguson, John. 1887. *Ceylon in the Jubilee Year*, 3rd edn. Colombo, John Haddon; London and A.M.J. Ferguson.

Fernando, C.M. 1907. 'History of Ceylon', In Arnold Wright (ed.) *Twentieth Century Impressions of Ceylon. Its History, People, Commerce, Industries and Resources*, London, Lloyds Great Britain Publishing Co.

Fuss, D. 1995. 'Fashion and the Homospectatorial Look'. In Kwame Appiah and Henry Louis Gates Jr (eds.) *Identities*. Chicago, Chicago University Press: pp.90–114.

Geiger, W. 1950. *The Mahavamsa*. Transl. Government Information Department. Colombo.

Guruge, A. (ed.) 1963. *Dharmapala Lipi*. Colombo, Government Press.

———.(ed.) 1965. *Anagarika Dharmapala. Return to Righteousness*, Colombo, Government Press.

143

Harris, E. 1994. *The Gaze of the Coloniser. British Views of Local Women in Nineteenth Century Sri Lanka*. Colombo, SSA.

Hochshild, Adam. 1988. *King Leopold's Ghost*. New York, Houghton Miflin Company.

Hendrickson, Hildi. 1996. *Clothing and Difference. Embodied Identities in Colonial and Post-Colonial Africa*. Durham, Duke University Press.

Karunanayake, N. (ed.) 1996. *The Press in Sri Lanka. Towards a Sound Policy Framework*. Nugegoda, Media Publications.

Kemper, Stephen. 1991. *The Presence of the Past. Chronicles, Politics and Culture in Sinhala Life*. New York, Cornell University Press.

Le Goff, Jacques. 1988. *Histoire-et-Memoire*. Paris, Gallimard.

Jayawardena, V.K. *The Rise of the Labour Movement in Ceylon*, Colombo, Sanjiva Prakashana.

Knox, R. 1958. *An Historical Relation of Ceylon*. repr., Dehiwela, Tisara Prakasakayo.

Malalgoda, Kithsiri. 1976. *Buddhism in Sinhalese Society, 1750–1900: A Study of Religious Revival and Change*. Berkeley and Los Angeles, University of California Press.

Metcalf, T.R. 1994. *Ideologies of the Raj, The New Cambridge History of India*, III, 4. Cambridge, Cambridge University Press.

Nandy, A. 1984. *The Intimate Enemy. Loss and Recovery of Self under Colonialism*. New Delhi, Oxford University Press.

———.1987. *Traditions, Tyranny and Utopias in the Politics of Awareness*. Delhi, Oxford University Press.

Nora, Pierre (ed.) 1997. *Les Lieux de Memoire*. Paris, Gallimard.

Peebles, P. 1995. *Social Change in Nineteenth-Century Sri Lanka*, Delhi, Navrang.

Percival, R. 1990. *An Account of the Island of Ceylon, 1803*. New Delhi, Asian Educational Services.

Perniola, V. 1983. *The Catholic Church in Sri Lanka The Dutch Period, Vol. II, 1712–1746*. Dehiwela, Tisara Prakaskayo.

Plate *Ceylon Annual*, 1932.

Prost, Antoine. 1996. *Douze Lecons sur L'Histoire*. Paris, Seuil.

Roach, M.E. and J.B. Eicher (eds.) 1965. *Dress, Adornment and the Social Order*. New York, John Wiley and Sons.

Roberts, M. (ed.) 1972. *Documents of the Ceylon National Congress and Nationalist Politics in Ceylon 1929–1950*, Vol.I, Sri Lanka, Colombo, National Archives.

————.(ed.) 1977. *Documents of the Ceylon National Congress and Nationalist Politics in Ceylon, 1929–1950*, Vol. II, Sri Lanka, Colombo, National Archives.

————.1994. 'The Imperialism of Silence under the British Raj: Arresting the Drum'. In Michael Roberts (ed.) *Exploring Confrontation. Sri Lanka: Politics, Culture and History*. (Switzerland), Harwood Academic Publishers: pp.149–81.

————.1997. 'Problems of Collective Identity in a Multi-Ethnic Society: Sectional Nationalism Vs. Ceylonese Nationalism, 1900–1940'. In M. Roberts (ed.) *Collective Identities Revisited* Vol. 1. Colombo, Marga Institute: pp.439–60.

————.1997. 'Elite Formation and Elites, 1832–1931'. In M. Roberts (ed.) *Collective Identities Revisited*, Vol.1, Colombo, Marga Institute: pp.191–265.

Rogers, J.D. 1987. *Crime, Justice and Society in Colonial Sri Lanka*. London, Curzon Press.

Royal Asiatic Society, Interim Report Royal Asiatic Society, 1897.

Ryan, B. 1953. *Caste in Modern Ceylon*. New Brunswick, Rutgers University Press.

Sarkar, N.K. 1957. *The Demography of Ceylon*. Colombo.

Smith, R.S. 1986. 'Rule by Records and Rule by Reports: Complementary Aspects of the British Imperial Rule by Law'. In V. Das (ed.) *The Word and the World*. New Delhi, Sage: pp.153–76.

Turner, L.J.B. 1927. *Handbook of Commercial and General Information for Ceylon*, H. Ross Cottle, Government Printer, Ceylon.

Weiner, A. and J. Schneider (eds.) 1989. *Cloth and Human Experience*. Washington D.C., Smithsonian Institute Press.

Wickramasinghe, Martin. 1961. *Upandasita*. Dehiwela, Tisara Publishers.

Wilson, A.J. 1988. *The Break-Up of Sri Lanka. The Sinhalese–Tamil Conflict*. London, C. Hurst and Company.

Wright, A. 1907. *Twentieth-Century Impressions of Ceylon. Its History, People, Commerce, Industries and Resources*. London, Lloyd's Greater Britain Publishing Co.

Journals and Periodicals

Alwis, A. 1920. 'Combs. Uses and Users'. *Ceylon Antiquary and Literary Register*, 6 (2), October. pp.100–101.

Anthonisz, R.G. 1908. 'The Dutch Burgher Union of Ceylon'. *Journal of the Dutch Burgher Union of Ceylon*, Vol.1.

————.1908. 'The Constitution and By-Laws of the Dutch Burgher Union of Ceylon'. *Journal of the Dutch Burgher Union of Ceylon*, Vol.1: pp.52–60.

————.1927. 'The Burghers of Ceylon'. *Journal of the Dutch Burgher Union of Ceylon*, 17, (1), July.

Breckenbridge, C.A. 1989. 'The Aesthetics and Politics of Colonial Collecting: India at the World Fairs'. *Comparative Studies in Society and History*, Vol. 31, No. 2: pp.195–216.

Campbell, C. 1996. 'The Meaning of Objects and the Meaning of Actions'. *Journal of Material Culture*, Vol. I, No. I: pp.93–105.

Coomaraswamy, E. 1906. 'Old Sinhalese Embroidery'. *Ceylon National Review*, Vol. I. No. 2, July: pp.119–29.

Fernando, C.M. 1906. 'Costume of the Sinhalese Ladies before the Portuguese Period'. *Spolia Zeylanica* 4 (14 & 15) December: p.142.

Gunasekere, V. 1932. *Young Ceylon.* May.

Gunawardena, R.A.L.H. 1979. 'The People of the Lion. The Sinhala Identity and Idealogy in History and Historiography'. *Sri Lanka Journal of Humanities*, Vol. 5, Nos. 1&2: pp.1–36.

Kotalawela, D.A. 1987. 'Some Aspects of Social Change in the South-East of Sri Lanka *c.*1700–1833. *Social Science Review, Studies in the Social History of Sri Lanka*: pp. 53–100.

146 Kuper, Hilda. 1973. 'Costume and Identity'. *Comparative Studies in Society and History*: pp. 348–67

Lorenzen, N. 1999. 'Who Invented Hinduism'. *Comparative Studies in Society and History*, Vol. 41, No. 4, October: pp. 630–59.

Masselos, June 1996. 'India's Republic Day: The Other 26 January'. *South Asia*, Vol. XIX, Special Issue: pp. 183–204.

Media, F. 1972. 'A Short History of Fashion in Ceylon'. *The Radio Times*: pp. 3, 12, 20.

Panditaratne, B.L. 1964. 'Trends of Urbanisation in Ceylon 1901–1953'. *The Ceylon Journal of Historical and Social Studies*, Vol. 7, No. 2, July–December: pp. 203–13.

Rabine, Leslie W. 1997. 'Not a Mere Ornament: Tradition, Modernity, and Colonialism in Kenyan and Western Clothing'. *Fashion Theory. The Journal of Dress, Body and Culture*, Vol.1, Issue 2, June: pp.145–68.

Rajanayagam, Dagmar Hellmann. 1989. 'Arumuka Navalar. Religious Leader or Social Reformer of Eelam'. *Indian Economic and Social History Review*, 26: pp. 235–57.

Unpublished Sources

Phyllis M. Martin. 1990. 'Christians and Clothing in French Congo'. *African History Seminar*, 28 November, School of Oriental and African Studies.

Photographs and charts

Bethia N. and Heather M. Bell: *H.C.P. Bell, Archaeologist of Ceylon and The Maldives*. Denbigh, Archetype Publishers. 1993.
  H.C.P. Bell and his labour force.

Ceylon Government Gazette. Part I (General). 17 April 1935
  Uniform for Muslims.
  Uniform for Kandyan Sinhalese.

E.B. Denham: *Ceylon at the Census of 1911*. Colombo 1912.
  Ceylon Races.

Lake House Archives
  S.W.R.D. Bandaranaike in national dress in the State Council, 1936.
  S.W.R.D. Bandaranaike at the *chakra* as a young man.
  D.S. Senanayake in top hat, 1948.
  Independence Day, 4 February 1948.

R.K. de Silva: *Early Prints of Ceylon (rpt 1984)*
  Sinhalese women picking coffee.
  A Sinhalese man and woman.

Arnold Wright (ed.), *Twentieth Century Impressions of Ceylon. Its History, People Commerce, Industries and Resources*, London, Lloyds Great Britain Publishing Co. 1907.
  A native Blacksmith (cover).
  Kandyan family, lady in osariya.
  Mudaliyar from the low country.
  Kandyan Mudaliyar.
  A Malay.
  A Muslim 'Tamby', commonly referred to as a Moor.
  D. A.L. Perera reproducing the Sigiriya frescoes.

INDEX

Dinapata Pravrutti, 61
discipline, 54
disobedience, 11
distinctiveness, 22, 85
diversity, 71
Dolahapillai, U.B., 65
domesticity, 54
Don Juan Dharmapala, a Sinhalese King, 35
Donoughmore, 18, 84, 85
dress, 9, 11, 21, 70
   of chiefs: official authenticities, 79–81
   etiquette, 80
   a mode of non-verbal communication, 2
   in a multi-ethnic society, 126
   an object of consumption, 124
   and politics, 124–5
   power, 127
   traditional, 58
Duchess of Kent, 36
Duke of Gloucester, 32
Duravas, 78
Dutch, 71
   puritanical, influence, 15
   restrictive regulations, 80
Dutch Burgher Union of Ceylon, 85
Dutch East India Company, 72, 81
Dutch Reformed Church, 33
Dutugemunu, King, 13
dying industry and British textiles, 45–7

economic, economy, 2
   opportunities, 51
   reasons to adopt the national dress, 21
Elara, 89
English textiles, 58
Enlightenment, 5

ethnic communities, 39
   costumes, 22
   groups and dress, 13, 22, 36, 75
ethnicity, 27, 49, 85
Eurasians, 77, 85
European, Europeans, 22, 75, 99, 116, 118
   culture, 11, 87
   style of dress and clothing, 11, 58
evangelism, 12
exoticism, 101

Fagan, Lt, 104
fashion, 2, 22, 53, 58–59, 60, 68n, 126
Ferguson, John, 31, 46–47
Fernando, W.M., 105, 117
festivals, 54
Foe, De, 102
food habits, 54–55
footwear, 81–82, 124
Forbes, H., 112
foreign goods, resistance to, 61
Foucault, 87
France, French
   national day, 24
   prejudices, 89
franchise, 60
Frazer, Reverend A.J., 14
frescoes, 112, 113–115, 117
furniture, 52–55

Gandhi, M.K., 23, 26, 30, 57, 63
gender difference, 49, 126
gendering authenticity, 86–90
Ghana Museum, 36
Ghana
   imperial fetes, 36
   independence, 36
   national day, 24
Goonetileke, Oliver, 21, 32

Gordon, Arthur, 87, 104, 106, 113
Governmental Oriental Library, Sri Lanka, 104
Goyigamas, 78, 86–87, 103
    state patronage, 78
Graff, Vander, 72
Gregory, William, 34–35
groups, 74–75
    boundaries, 82
Guevara, Che, 127
Gunananda, Mohottivatte, 12

Haldummulla, Sri Lanka, 64
half castes, 71
Hambantota, Sri Lanka
    rubber mania, 50
Hammaru, 77
Hannalis, 56
harbour, 33–5
Harischandra, Walisinha, 12, 64
Harris, Elisabeth, 91
heritages, 5
Hewavitarne, C.A., 47
Hewavitharana Weaving School, Colombo, 65
hierarchical status, 60
Hinduism, 12
History
    as exhibit, 35–6
    as memory, 100–1
Hitopadesa, 102
Hocart, A.M., 110
housing patterns, 51–2
Howard, John, 32
humanity, 5
hygiene, 53, 54

identity, identities, 2, 11, 22, 70–72, 78, 124, 125
    politics, 85–86
image, 9
imports, imported goods, 48–49, 60
    condemnation, 63

independence day celebration, 26, 27, 38
India, Indian
    compromise on dress, 125
    imperial rule of law, 74
    influence, 62
    labour, 119
    Moors, 77
    National Day, 23
    Tamils, 77
    women, style of dress, 11, 125
Indonesia
    national dress, 14
Industrial Revolution, 46
industries, traditional, 64–67
Islam, 12, 126

Jaffna, 35
    Tamils, 86, 126
Janatha Vimukthi Perumuna (JVP), 126, 127
Jansz, G.E., 102
Javanese, 85
Jayasuriya, Chandrasekera Ananda Prasanna Warnakula, 27
Jayasuriya, Charles Andrew Perera Warnakula, 27
Jayewardene, J.R., 21, 32, 126
Jennings, Ivor, 9
joie de vivre, 2, 112–13
Juta, See footwear
JVP, *See* Janatha Vimukthi Perumuna

kabakuruththuwa, 15
Kalutara, Sri Lanka, 51, 52
Kandy, King of, 33
Kandy Herald, 102
Kandyans, Kandyan kingdom, chiefs, 15–16, 17, 73, 77, 80, 82–84, 124
    costumes, 22

153

155

157